Studies in Literature
and
Literary Theory

Studies in Literature *and* Literary Theory

M.A. (English)

According to Syllabus in Major Indian Universities

SANGITA MEHTA
M.A., M. Phil. Ph.D.*
Asstt. Prof. in Haryana College of
Technology & Management, Kaithal

REKHA CHUTANI
M.A., M.Phil, B. Ed.,
Lect. in Haryana College of
Technology & Management, Kaithal

ADHYAYAN

Adhyayan Publishers & Distributors
New Delhi-110002

Published by
ADHYAYAN PUBLISHERS & DISTRIBUTORS
4378/4 B, 105, J.M.D. House, Murari Lal Street
Ansari Road, Darya Ganj, New Delhi-110002
Ph. : 011-23263018, 011-23277156, Fax : 011-23280028
E-mail : adhyayanpublishers@yahoo.com

Studies in Literature and Literary Theory

Edition : 2011
ISBN : 978-81-8435-268-9

Printed in India

Published by Harish Chandra Yadav for Adhyayan Publishers & Distributors, Laser Typesetting at Net Graphics and Printed at Tarun Offset Printers, Delhi.

Dedicated to the Pillar of Life—"Ma"

Acknowledgment

One can't deny the fact that Literature has always fascinated the people. It has gained a great importance in the context of present day globalisation environment. We are grateful to all those who contributed to bring out this effort by encouraging us in this noble-mission. First of all, we are thankful to Almighty God who always showers his blessings on us. We are grateful to the Managing Committee of HCTM, Kaithal specially to Er. G.K. Sethi ji, the Managing Director and Dr. H.C. Sharma, the head of the Deptt. who encouraged us for the research work and provided all the facilities to complete this work. We are also thankful to Dr. Ajay Sharma, who always guided us. We acknowledge our indebtedness to Jawaharlal Nehru Library, Kurukshetra University, Kurukshetra, Punjab University Chandigharh and Library of HCTM for making requisite material readily available.

Last but not the least we are thankful to our publisher. Adhyayan Publications, to publish this book.

Authors

Preface

We take pleasure in presenting the first edition of "Studies in Literature and Lirary theory" for M.A. Final year.

This book follows syllabus prescribed in majar Indian universities.

We hope that this book will definitely be helpful and motivating to the students of literature for the examination point of view as well as for different competitive exams like UGC-NET. The book focuses on all the important elements of literature. It has been tried at its best to provide the material in a very easy and comprehensible manner. It is expected that this book will overcome all the problems facing by the students of literature and will work as a shield to the students. We are sure that we will be successful in providing a supporting hand to the young minds, after all the future belongs to you my dear students. I am grateful to the publisher 'Adhyayan Publishers & Distributors' for the keen interest they have taken and the co-operation, they extended to us, in publishing this book.

Contents

Fourth Semester
Critical Theory (Part II)

1. T.S. Eliot's The Function of Criticism
2. E.M. Forster on Flat and Round Characters
3. Foster on "Point of View"
4. W.K. Wimsat and M.C. beardslay on "The International Fallacy"
5. Wimsatt and Beardslay on '"The Affective Fallacy"
6. Raymond Williams, Realism and the Contemporary Novel"
7. Lionel Trilling's Fraud and Literature.
8. Psychological Criticism
9. Post Structuralism
10. New-Historicism

T.S. Eliot's The Function of Criticism

The essay Function of Criticism, (1923) arose out of a controversy. T.S. Eliot's essay 'Tradition and Individual Talent' was published a few years earlier in 1919.

Middleton Murry Challenged the opinions of Eliot in his essay 'Romanticism and the Tradition.' The present essay is Eliot's reply to Murry. The essay is divided into four parts.

Eliot begins the essay by referring to certain views he had expressed in his earlier essay, Tradition and Individual Talent', because they are relevant to the present essay. In the earlier essay he has pointed out that there is an intimate relation between the present and the past in the world of literature. The entire literature of Europe, from Homer down to the present day, forms a literary tradition and it is in relation to this tradition that individual writers and individual works of art have their significance. Eliot defines criticism as. "The commentation and exposition of works of art by means of written words." Since the end of criticism is clear and well-defined it should be easy to determine whether a critic has performed his function well or not. The difficulty arises from the fact that critics, instead of trying to discipline their personal prejudices and whims and composing their differences with as many of their fellow-critics as possible and cooperating in the common pursuit of true judgement. Express extreme views, the ways in which they differ from others. The result is that criticism becomes like a Sunday Park full of orators competing with each other to attract as large an audience as possible.

In the second part of the essay, Eliot digresses into a consideration of Middleton Murry's views on classicism and romanticism. Murry makes a clear distinction between the two and says that one cannot be a classic and a romantic at one and the same time. In this respect Eliot praises Murry but he does not agree with him when he makes the issue a national and radical issue. In his views the difference between classicism and romanticism is, "the difference between the complete and the fragmentary, the adult and the immature, the orderly and the Chaotic." To him the concept of the 'inner voice' sounds remarkably like doing.

In the third part of the essay, Eliot summarily dismisses the views of Murry. The tone is one of light ridicule. He contemptuously calls the inner voice whiggery. For those who believe in the 'inner voice', criticism is of no value at all because the function of criticism is to discover some common principles for achieving perfection in art.

In the fourth part, Eliot deals with the problem of criticism in all its manifold aspects. In the very beginning, he comments upon the terms 'critical' and 'creative' Eliot expresses the view that the criticism exployed by a writer on his own work is the most vital and highest kind of criticism. Eliot calls such criticism, 'Workshop Criticism'. It is a mistake to separate critical and creative activities. A large part of creation is in reality criticism. But critical writing cannot be creative. The critical activity finds its highest fulfillment when it is fused with creation, with the labour of the artist.

Eliot next proceeds to consider the qualifications of a critic. The foremost quality which an ideal critic must have is a highly developed sense of fact. Comparison and analysis are the chief tools of a critic. A critic must use these tools with care and intelligence. The critic should approach the work of art with a free mind, unprejudiced by any theories or preconceived notions.

Critic is like a scientist working with an open mind and co-operating with others for the realisation of truth, which he knows can only be tentative and the function of criticism is to educate taste, to promote enjoyment and understanding of literature.

E.M. Forster—Flat and Round Character

Edward Morgan Forster (1879-1970) was an Anglo-Indian writer. His experience in India produced his most celebrated novel. 'A passage to India' published in 1924. The novel is considered as his masterpiece and one of the finest English novels of the twentieth century. His Aspects of the Novel (1927) presents Forster's theoretical pronouncements on the novel. According to him, the fundamental aspect of novel is a story-telling aspect. He admits that the novelist may be interested in character and motive, in some social and moral problem or in the landscape involving the atmosphere of mind and feeling. Forster considers second aspect of novel as people. In this aspect the novelist's appeals to intelligence and imagination and the focus is on : to whom did it happen. The characters on the pages of the novel are made up of words while a real life, they are flesh and blood creatures. The characters in the novel are completely known because their creator knows them completely. In real life we cannot understand people completely because their secret thoughts and feelings are hidden from us. Thus in a character in the novel the reader enjoys a kind of reality that we can never get it in real life.

Characters are of two types—Flat and Round, Flat characters were called 'humorous' in the seventeenth century. They are also called "types" or "caricatures". A flat character is built round a single idea or quality and remains stable and unchanged. Forster quotes example of Mrs. Micabwar (David Copperfield). She says she won't desert Mr. Micabwar and she does not. Thus lack of complexity, change or growth is the essence of flat characters. Flat characters are easily manageable and recognizable and the reader can easily achieve emotional identification with them. The reader can easily achieve emotional identification with them. The reader can easily remember them afterwards but the flat character which is serious and tragic is apt to be a bore. It is not as great achievement as the round character. That's why Forster rates Jane Austen's round characters higher than Dickens' Flat characters. He admits that the vitality of Dickens' characters is not because of his art but a 'conjuring trick'.

The Round Characters are capable of growth and change. Therefore, they are capable of surprising us in a convincing way. If a character does not surprise and convince. It is a flat character pretending to be round. Forster remarks that Jane Austen transforms even a flat character like Mrs. Bertram (Mansfield Park) into a round character. According to him all characters in Jane Austen, Dostovesky and all main character of War and Peace are round.

Forster is more concerned with the author's ability to portray life.

Forster's Point of View

Edward Morgan Forster was born on January 1,1879. The origin and position of his family, which belonged to the 'intellectual aristocracy' of the British Middle class, had a considerable influence on his development. Forster as a novelist has achieved considerable success and popularity. But he is not regarded as one of the great moderns and has been refused the status of James Joycee, Henry James, D.H. Lawrence etc. who are great discoverers of modern fiction. His works are characterized by high quality of thought and literary excellence. He wrote not only novels but also short stories, biographies, travel books, essays and books of literary criticism. There are however, some set themes on which he wrote, the conflict of cultures, the disastrous impact to materialism and provincialism, the cult of personal relationship, the need for international outlook and love. In all his works, like *where Angels Fear to Tread* (1905), The Longer Journey (1907), *A Room with a view* (1908), *Howards End* (1910), A passage to India (1942), *Aspects of the Novel* (1927), Forester is seen as seriously reflecting on the ultimate truths of life and universe.

The problem of 'Point of view' or "the position from which the action of the novel is presented," as Jacques Souvage defines it in 'An Introduction to the study of the novel, is one that has engaged critics right from the time of Plato. The basic distinction is very important for the analysis of the point of view in fiction. The term was used early as July, 1866 in the British Quarterly Review. Henry James felt that the point of view was the means by which he could achieve the required intensity and coherence in his novels. But Forster does not attach undue importance to the point of view. In his work Aspects of the Novel, he elaborates certain principles or aspects of novel as a creative writing. He does not approach his subject oronologically by tracing the development of the novel. He accepts the truth in : "History develops, arts stand still". He considers seven aspects of the novel : the story, the Plot, the fantasy, the prophecy, Pattern, Rhythm and the character. The novel must tell a story and suspense should be there to keep the reader awake. We also discusses the point of view to be used in presenting a character. He cautions that I novelist, "should not betray too much interest in his own methods". It is not necessary for a novelist to stick to one point of view, he can shift point of view when needed. What ever method the novelist uses, for successful characterization, he must be able to "bounce the reader in accepting what he says". Forster believes that the novel can also include the plot which is different from the story and Fantasy is an aspect of fiction that makes an extra demand. Prophecy in Forster's point of view is a 'tone of voice', a special "accent in the novelist's voice", which makes the theme universal. Forster says that pattern and Rhythm also belong to the aesthetic aspect of a novel. So the pattern should not be too rigid but rhythm should be there.

W.K. Wimsatt and Beardsley's 'The Intentional Fallacy'

Intentional Fallacy is an important term in New Criticism. This important principle was first used by W.K. Wimsatt and Monroe Bearsley in their essay. 'The Intentional Fallacy (1946). The phrase 'intentional fallacy' is ambiguous. Many critics have different interpretations of it. Wimsatt and Bearsley Claim that in order to understand the full meaning of a text, One must lay aside all possible intentions of the author and concentrate on the text itself. Although a literary work has an individual author, that fact should not distract the reader from exploring the public meaning accessible through the organic structure of the text. The reader should reject the idea of an author's intention in order to attain an understanding. Both Wimsatt and beardsley affirm that, "the poem is not the critic's own and not the author's." The works exist for readers to examine : its merits, demerits, language and content are public knowledge. The reader should discard any concern about the author's intentions or reasoning. The writers divide the evidence used in making interpretations of literary texts into three categories.

1. Internal evidence—It is the first most reliable and most accessible type of evidence for the meaning of a piece of literature. It is discovered through the semantics and syntax of the work. It is not only found within the text itself but also comprises elements of the structure of the text. The form of epic poetry, the meter, quotations etc. are internal to the work.

2. External evidence—Like internal evidence it can also be available for observation. It is less accessible and less valuable. It is directly concerned with what the artist may have intended to do when it is not clean from the work itself.

3. Contextual Evidence—The third kind of evidence concerns any meaning derived from the specific work's relationship to other art made by this particular artist. Wimsatt and beardsley team it as 'intermediate' evidence. This evidence is "about the character of an author or about private or semiprivate meanings attached to words or topics by an author.

The International Fallacy, according to Wimsatt and Beardsley grows out of a romantic dealing with private, idiosyncratic elements of literary composition. The critical reader must look to a text as a self-defining work that is unified by a variety of literary elements.

Wimsatt and Beardsley on 'The Affective Fallacy'

The term 'Affective Fallacy' was coined by W.K. Wimsatt and Monroe Beardsley as a principle of New Criticism. It is used to refer to the assumed error of judging or evaluating a text on the basis of its emotional effects on a reader. Wimsatt and Beardsley coined the concept of Affective Fallacy to give an answer to the idea of impressionistic criticism which argues that the reader's response to a poem is the ultimate indication of its value. Wimsatt anticulated the concept of affective fallacy in The Verbal Icon (Collection of essays, 1954). Wimsatt was a literary critic who joined the English department at yale University in 1939. Where he taught until he died in 1975. Beardley was a philosopher of art and aesthetics. As a staunch formalist critic, Wimsatt believed in the authority of the poem and that any analysis of a poem must center on the text itself.

The Affective Fallacy is a confusion between the poem and its results. Wimsatt used the team to refer to all forms of criticism that understood a text's effect upon the reader to be the primary route to analyzing the importance and success of that text. This definition of the fallacy includes nearly all of the major modes of literary criticism prior to the 20th century. "The Affective Fallacy is a confusion between the poem and its results (what it is and what is does), a special case of epistemological skepticism (which) begins by trying to derive the standard of criticism from the psychological effects of the poem and ends in impressionism and relativism (with the result that) the poem itself, as an object of specifically critical judgement, tends to disappear."

2. The report of some readers....that a poem or story induces in them vivid images, intense feelings or heightened consciousness is neither anything which can be refuted nor anything which it is possible for the objective critic to take into account.

3. The critic is not a contributor to statistical countable reports about the poem, but a teacher or explicator of meanings. His readers, if they are alert will not be content to take what he says as testimony, but will scrutinize it as teaching.

As with many concepts of New Criticism, the concept of the affective fallacy was both controversial and widely influential, never accepted wholly by any great number of critics.

Raymond Williams Realism and the Contemporary Novel

Raymond Williams was a figure of extraordinary dominance in Britain across a wide range not only in literary and cultural inquiry but of intellectual and political opposition as well. He was a multiple author of seven novels, a number of plays and two dozen more than academic books. He was to become one of Britain's greatest post war cultural historians, theorists and polemicists. He is influential in various fields. English studies, sociology, politics and cultural and media studies. His work has generated research in different areas.

Williams says that the novel is not so much a literary form as a whole literature itself within the wide boundaries, there is room for almost every kind of contemporary writing. Great harm is done to the tradition of fiction and to the necessary critical discussion of it, If "the novel" is equated with any one kind of prose work. He states that it is a fact that this tradition, as a tradition has broken down. But I don't mean, of course, to tie it to any particular style. He offers fourfold classification social description, social formula, personal description, personal formula—as a way of beginning any general analysis of the contemporary novel. Finally he made the judgement in an arbitrary way in this brief account, though in fact the detailed analysis came first and it was only later that he saw this classification emerging. He says that there are certain immediate clarifying factors. The realistic novel needs, obviously, a genuine community : a community of persons linked not merely by one kind of relationship-work, friendship, family-but by many, interlocking kinds. It is obviously difficult in our society, to find a community of this sort. He says that realistic novel is so important. We need the recovery of wholeness, for the most ordinary business in experience can only take place in ways which the realistic novel alone can record. If the recovery could be set down here in a formula, the position would be different. But it can only be set down, if at all, in the whole terms, which the realistic novel makes possible. Where all the persons are of absolute value in themselves and where their qualities are the qualities of the commonway of life. The stages to their will be slow, but there, I think, is the direction in experience which may again transform the novel.

Lionel Trilling's Freud and Literature

Lionel Trilling (1905-1975) was an American literary critic, author and educator. He published two complex studies of authors Mathew Arnold (1939) and E.M. Forster (1943), both written in response to a concern with 'the tradition of humanistic thought and the intellectual middle class which believes it continues this tradition. Lionel trilling argues that the Freudian approach to psychology is the "only systematic account of the human mind" which is comparable "in point of subtlety and complexity, of interest and tragic power" to the "mass of psychological insights which literature has accumulated through the centuries." Psychoanalysis has had a great impact on the study of literature has accumulated through the centuries." Psychoanalysis has had a great impact on the study of literature. The effect is "reciprocal', greater than the effect of literature upon Freud. Freud himself admitted, the "poets and philosophers before me uncovered the unconscious". Trilling summarises his arguments by saying that his point has been that "Freud's ideas could tell us something about it "but that 'Freud's very conception of art is inadequate". Trilling suggests, Freud is very aware of the limits of the 'application of the analytic method to specific works of art", However, freud does believe that it accomplishes two things. "explain the inner meanings of the work of art and explain the temperament of the artist as man. What Freud and Jones asserted is that

'What Shakespeare intended to say is that Hamlet cannot act because he is incapacitated by the guilt he feels at his unconscious attachment to his mother. Trilling then turns his attention to the view that an artwork reveals much about the mind of the artist which in turn shades light on the artwork.

In beyond the pleasure principle (1920), Trilling contends, Freud offers both a 'speculative attempt to solve a perplexing problem in clinical analysis". And an important contribution to the study of catharsis in tragedy a la Aristotle. Freud stumbles here upon certain facts that contradict his earlier theory that all dreams, "have the intention of fulfilling the dreamer's wishes. They are in the service of what Freud calls the pleasure principle which is opposed to the reality principle'. Freud offers a vision of man and his desire for man is that he should be human and to this end his science is devoted.

Psychological Criticism

The word 'criticism' is derived from the Greek meaning 'Judgement'. It means criticism is the exercise of judgement on the works of literature.

It is the play of the mind on a work of literature and its basic function is to examine its good and bad qualities and finally to evaluate its artistic value. According to Atkins, criticism is the play of the mind on the aesthetic qualities of literature, having for its object an interpretation of literary values. Saintsbury says that the criticism busies itself, "with the goodness or badness, the success or ill success, of literature form the purely literary point of view." There is a bewildering multiplicity of views and theories regarding the scope, definition and the function of literary criticism. There are various types of criticism that have been flourished from time to time like legislative criticism, Judicial Criticism, Theoretical Criticism, Evaluative Criticism, Historical Criticism, Bio-graphical Criticism, Comparative Criticism, Descriptive Criticism, Impressionistic Criticism, Ontological Criticism, Sociological Criticism, Archetypal criticism, and Psychological Criticism.

Psychological criticism means which discovers the hidden significance and brings new interpretations. It enables the critic to study the inner life, inner dreams and desires. Through this criticism we can also find out the hidden meaning of a work in addition to the surface meaning. It can also be helpful in interpreting the fictitious characters. I.A. Richard is the first rate critic since coleridge who used this psychological criticism. It is only because of his interest in psychology which made him a critic with a difference. He applies his psychological approach to bring out the mental equilibrium. Whenever he feels a conflict between inner desires and the reality while evaluating a work of literature.

Psychological criticism focuses primarily on the characters and on what psychological forces influence and shape them throughout the work. It is the application of psychoanalysis within literature. The psychonalysis means a group of theories which concern the relationship between the conscious and the unconscious. Psychological criticism aims to reveal these profound and myterious concepts in the literary field. Through this psychomatic approach one is able to allow the possibility of understanding and gathering the in depths insights of literature. This through this process we can come to know about those numerous beliefs, feelings and views in an individual's head that the rest of the world is simply not aware of.

Post Structuralism

Post structuralism is based on the linguistic theories of Ferdinand de Saussure and the deconstructionist theories of Jacques Derrida. A conspicuous announcement to American scholars of the post structural point of view was Jacques Derrida's paper on "Structure, Sign and Play in the Discourse of the Human Sciences' delivered in 1966 to an international colloquium at John Hopkins University. (The paper is included in Derrida's writing and difference, 1978. Derrida attacked the systematic, quasi-scientific pretensions of the strict from a structuralism-derived from saussure's concept of the structure of language and represented by the cultural anthropologist Claude Levistrauss by asserting that the notion of a systemic structure, whether linguistic or other presupposes a fixed 'center' that serves to organize and regulate the structure. Yet itself escapes structurality.

Poststructuralists do not support the traditional western insistence on a single correct reading of a text. Writers associated with the movement are Roland Earthes, Jacques Lacan, Julia Kristeva and Michel Fouccault. There is not a clear-cut division between structuralism and poststructuralism in practice. Structuralism encompasses approaches to criticism which use linguistic models to enable critics to focus not on the inherent meaning of a work but on the structure which produce or generate meaning. Post structuralist focuses on the ways in which the texts themselves subvert this enterprise; the structuralist emphasis on difference as constructing relatively stable systems of meaning is displaced in post-structuralism by Derrida's concept of difference in french term which puns on the words for difference and deferral thus suggesting the endless displacement of unstable meaning along a chain of signifies.

New Historicism

New Historicism that developed in 1980's and gained widespread influence in the 1990s. is a school of literary theory, grounded in critical theory. It came into existence through the work of the critic stephen greenblatt. The primary aim of New Historicists is to understand the work through its historical context and to understand cultural and intellectual history through literature which shows the new discipline of the history of ideas. New Historicists tend to draw on the disciplines of political science and anthropology given their interest in governments, institutions and culture. They are like the cultural Materialists interested in questions of circulation, negotiation, profit and exchange, i.e. how activities that purport to be above the market (including literature) are infact informed by the values of that market. New Historicists take this position future by then claiming that all cultural activities may be considered as equally important texts for historical analysis. New Historicism is more specifically concerned with questions of power and culture.

The difficulty of introducing this school is that a number of different approaches to history and culture. It often get lamped together under the category of 'New Historicism.' Some of the most prominent New Historicists like Stephen greenblat and Alan Liu, Either reject or antique the very term. "New Historicism." New Historicism shares many of the same theories with cultural Materialism while in its political interpretations. It is indebted to Marxism. Marxism tends to see literature as part of a superstructure in which the 'economic base' manifests itself while New Historicist thinkers tend to take a more nuanced view of power. They see it not as class related but extend throughout society. Michael Foucault in his work, 'Critical Theory' Discusses about New Historicism and Marxism. Foucault had the ability to pick up common terms and give them new meaning, thus changing the way critics addressed such pervasive issues as 'power', 'discourse', 'discipline', 'subjectivity, sexuality and government.

New Historicism has received criticism, particularly from postmodernists. New Historicism denies the 'post-modern' or 'post-historical' phase. The main reasons behind this criticism are that New Historicism unlike post-modernism, acknowledges that all historic views, accounts and facts they use contain biases which derive from the position of their view.

American Literature (Part II)

1. The Great Gatsby by F. Scott Fitzgerald
2. The Sound and the Fury by Faulkner
3. Herzog by Saul Bellow
4. Invisible Man by Ralph Ellison
5. Arthur Miller
6. Who's Afraid of Virginia Woolf by Abee
7. Sylvia Plath
8. Langston Hughes
9. Wallace Stevens
10. Catch 22 by Joseph Heller

The Great Gatsby by F. Scott Fitzgerald

Francis Scott Fitzgerald was born on September 22] 1896, in St. Paul, Minnesota. He was the only son of the upper middle class Catholic family. His family had the traditions of the upper middle class but the financial security was not there to keep these traditions alive. He also tried his career in athletics but ultimately found himself suitable for writing and got his three stories published in the Newsman News in 1911. Soon in 1913 in princeton, he began to work for the magazines like the Tiger, The Nassau lit, a serious literary magazine edited by Edmund Wilson, for whom Fitzgerald had a great respect. In the mean time he fell in love with a girl Ginreva king belonged to rich class of Chicago. But he couldn't attain her because of the gap of the status and the result was more seriousness in writing. Finally in 1921, he married Zelda, who also belonged to a wealthy Alabama family] only after getting recognization by getting his work **This Side of paradise** published. He moved into a luxury apartment in New York City with his wife after getting published his short stories titled **Flappers and Philosophers**. He received the most impressive critical appraisals, at the publication of the **The Great Gatsby** in 1925, the best of his works today.

Fitzgerald himself once said of **The Great Gatsby** that everything must contribute to the dramatic movement and the device of a first-person narrative is one of the ways in which this aim is achieved. It is a novel of ideas and is heavily dependent on symbolism. As a work of art it is able to make its own position on the basis of its own merits. In this work like all others, the money remains at the centre. It may be because of the lack of money in Fitzgerald's own life on the surface, it is a story of the love between a man and a woman. The main theme of the novel however covers a much larger scape. It is a highly symbolic meditation on 1920s America as a whole, in particular the disintegration of the American dream in an era of unprecedented prosperity and material excess. Fitzgerald portrays 1920s as an era of decayed social and moral values in the pursuit of wealth and pleasure. As Gatsby's dream of loving Daisy is distorted by the difference in their respective social status, his resorting to crime to make enough money to attain her, to impress her. But his dream is ruined just like the American Dream by the unworthiness of its object. When his dream distorts, the only option that is left for Gatzby is to die. And at last Nick, the narrator of the Gatsby and the confident of all moves back to Minnesota, where American values still exist.

The Sound and The Fury (1929)

The sound and the Fury is a novel written by the American author William Faulkner. It was Faulkner's fourth novel and was not immediately successful. The title of the novel is taken from Macbeth's Soliloquy in Act 5, scene 5 of William Shakespear's Macbeth. The novel has achieved great critical success and a prominent place among the greatest of American novels, often counted one of the 100 greatest books. It played a role in William Faulkner's receiving the 1949 Nobel Prize Literature.

The general outline of the story is the decline of the compson family, a once noble southern family descended from U.S. Civil War hero general compson. The family falls Victim to those Vices which Faulkner believed were responsible for the problems in the reconstructed South : racism, avarice, selfishness and the psychological inability of individuals to become determinants. Over the course of the thirty years or so related in the novel, the family falls into financial ruin, loses its religious faith and the respect of the town of Jefferson and many of them die tragically. Faulkner was very much preoccupied with the question of how the ideals of the old South could be maintained or preserved in the post-Civil War era. Seen in this light, the decline of the compson family might be interpreted as an examination of the corrosion of traditional morality only to be replaced by a modern helplessness.

The novel's appreciation has in large part been due to the technique of its construction, Faulkner's ability to recreate the thought patterns of the human mind. It was an essential development in the stream of consciousness narrative technique. There are also echoes of existential themes in the novel. In 1945, Faulkner wrote an appendix to the novel to be published in the then forthcoming anthology, The Portable Faulkner. Having been written sixteen years after The Sound and the Fury, the appendix presents some textual differences from the novel but serves to clarify the novel's opaque story.

Herzog by Saul Bellow

Saul Bellow's Herzog (1964) is a complicated and multifaceted novel. Saul Bellow, American writer and teacher is considered one of America's finest writers. Bellow often, writes about people who feel that they don't belong in the world they live in, who feel that they are outsiders and do not fit into the present environment full of absurdity and chaos as opposed to the intellectually and emotionally nourishing past. Bellow won Nobel Prize for literature in 1976 and National Medal of Arts in 1998. His best known works are The adventures of Augie March, (1953), Herzog (1964), and Humboldt's gift.(1975)

Herzog, after its publication became a bestseller cementing Saul Bellow's reputation with the public-as well as the critics. The novel has won praise for its penetrating, sometimes humorous, portrait of a middle aged man searching for meaning and selfhood in the anxietyridden America of the 1960s. The novel is a series of Fragmented reflections, often revealed in an epistolary, or letter format. Moses Herzog, the main character becomes obsessed with writing letters to everyone under the sun, living or deceased including his family, friends, enemies and historical figures. Over the past few months, He has experienced a spiritual and emotional paralysis triggered by the breakup of his marriage and his contemplation of the wasteland of modern life, "down in the mire of post-renaissance, post humanistic, post Cartesian dissolution, next door to the void." In the letters, Herzog examines and evaluates various philosophical theories, recalls fond images of his childhood, apologizes to ignored friends and lovers, and especially berate those like his wife and her lover, who have caused his sufferings. During the course of the novel, Herzog is forced to cope with his sense of alienation and displacement as he analyzies his past and tries to determine his future. By the end of the novel, his search has resulted in a tenuous, but nevertheless satistying restoration of his faith in himself and in humanity.

At the beginning of the novel, Herzog admits he has been engaged in a desperate search for meaning for insight into his own troubled existence and human existence in general. as he writes his letter he conducts that search, entering into dialogues with people who have made an impact on his life and others. Through this process he hopes to gain know ledge and acceptance of self.

Seymour Epstein in his article on Saul Bellow for The Denver Quarterly notes that the letters reflect a need, "to feel a passionate faith in some higher order, intelligence or idea that will do as medium through which one can seek transcendence."

The Invisible Man by Ralph Ellison

Ralph waldo Ellison born in Oklahoma city in 1914 was named after the famous American poet and philosopher Ralph waldo Emerson because his father Lewis Ellison wanted him to be a poet. From the very childhood days he was very good in playing trumpet and music. He got a recognization in the world of music and after getting a scholarship on the basis of music he joined the Tubegee Institute in Macon County, Alabama to study. Under the influence of works of Ernest Hemingway, George Bernard Shaw and T.S. Eliot he began to write essays, reviews and short stories and dropped the idea to study arts. Soon he came in contact with Langston Hughes and Richard wright and joined Federal writer's Project. He also worked in the Merchant Marine as a cook during world war II and this is the place when he wrote the first line of his world wide recognized work i.e. *The Invisible Man,* which made him won National Book Award in 1953. In his work he has said :

"I am invisible, understand simply because people refuse to see me" (The Invisible Man Prologue).

The invisible novel has covered many social issues like individuality and personal identity, black nationalism etc. It is the story of an unnamed African American man who considers himself invisible, he explains that the reason of invisibility is not the supernatural cause or the any accidental incidence. He is invisible because of the disinterest of the other people to notice him, as he is black. Even sometimes he feels doubt about himself whether he has the existence or not everybody sees him as a stereotype, not as a real person. The protagonist has lost his sense of identity in a world of prejudice and hostility. He has enclosed himself in an underground cellar which is lightened with 1,369 bulks in order to solve his relationship with the rest of the society.

As a young boy, the narrator overhears the last words of his dying grandfather, whose message always remains in his mind. But at every step of his life he feels that all the organizations have always manipulated their constituents. The narrator wants to show the effects of racism, because he himself has experienced the ignorance of white people as a black. His struggle involves the conflict between how others perceive him and how he perceives himself. Because of the racism, he was veined by others in terms of racial stereotypes—as a mugga, pumpkin or savage. But he desires recognization of individuality rather than recognization based on these stereotypes. He addresses the white man as blind, who are not able to see him as an individual that is the reason the narrator fees the outside world in search of freedom to define himself without the constraints that racism imposes. Through this novel he is not just taking about himself but the term 'invisibility' remains universally applicable for any group that is socially marginalized. What ultimately he emerged as a winner and his success can also be seen even today. In the present scenario the black Americans are more visible, as we see that Barrack Obama is the nation's first African American President.

Arthur Miller

There is no denying the fact that everybody wants to achieve success, everybody aspires to live a life full of dignity and respect. There is nothing wrong in these aspirations and ambitions. But the most important thing is the way through which one achieves success. The kind of success which is attained at the cost of family has hardly any value. On the contrary, the family which ignores society is equally culpable. There are many playwrights who have written their plays with this aim in mind. But one of the most important dramatists of the 20th century is, undoubtedly the American dramatist, Arthur Miller.

Arthur Miller was born in Harlem, on 17th October 1915. A jew by birth Miller attended a public school in Harlam, but his school life seems to have no strong impressions on his mind. He grew up during the years of the depression in America and this was the most important factor which determined his work. He is usually regarded as an intellectual dramatist that is, one whose plays express moral, social and political ideas. In themes, that prevently recur, Miller is strongly in favour of a positive relationship between the individual and the society. He argues against injustice, exploitation, competition, guilt, betrayal and vested private interest. His characters are people who try to escape the consequences of their actions, who try to declare their innocence even when their action involves guilt. The process of his plays is one that brings his characters into confrontation with themselves.

All My Sons (1947), Miller's first successful play won him the New York Drama Critics Circle Award. There is no doubt that All My Sons deserves a special place in playwright's Canon because it constitutes his first major theatrical achievement. He was also awarded with a Pulitzer prize for his most popular, powerful and affecting play Death of a Salesman in American Theatrical history, which was first produced on Feb. 10, 1949. It was also said that as the New Vorbers made their way to exit, their faces were stained with tears and their eyes revealed their inner depression. In just two hours Miller had succeeded in reminding them of their own guilt through simple images from the life of a salesman.

Miller's Protagonists dream for the impossible and unattainable. Their dreams are grounded in reality. But the problem with them is that they want two opposites in an instant. They cannot leave one thing for the other. For instance Joe Keller in All My Sons dreams of a happy and wealthy future for his family on one hand and social prestige on the other. But in earning too much for the prosperity of his own family he himself betrays the society and does not feel guilt. But at last he feels guilt for his crime. In the same way Willy Loman in Death of a Salesman wants to get success in the industria; capitalistic society as well as longs for the pastoral life. But his failure in one leads to his failure in the other.

For Miller Betrayal has always been the central concern, the betrayal of the individual by Social values, of the social values by its own necessities. He also shows that the modern man is becoming more and more individualistic day by day. He cannot think beyond himself and his family. For his family he betrays the society. But Miller says that a man's conscience can never be completely extinguished. When a man has committed a wrong, his conscience would certainly make him feel uneasy about it. This is exactly what Miller wants to depict in his plays that man is a social animal and cannot line in isolation. In an interview given to Jomes J. Martin, Miller said :

> "I think that man is a social animal, there is no getting away from it. He is in the society the way of fish is in the water, and the water is in the fish. I can not possibly disentangle them, because I am under no illusion that people really invent themselves.

Thus Miller wants to convey that in order to achieve happiness and fulfillment in life a balance has to struck between the individual thinking and the social actions. There should be a balance between dreams and obsessions of the individual and the harsh realities of the society. The individual should understand that the excessive desire for success brings disaster. The society, on the other hand, should understand the individual as an essential part of it. It is only by achieving and maintaining this balance that man can avoid the feeling of guilt, betrayal and the resultant suffering.

Who's Afraid of Virginia Woolf by Abee

Who's Afraid of Virginia Wold? is Edward Albee's masterpiece. Edward Franklin Albee, the renowned American dramatist has been adjudged as "our best playwright" by critics. He is widely acclaimed for his valuable contribution to American Drama. He gave it a new direction. Albee born on march 12, 1928 in Washington. He got the inspiration of writing from his boarding.

He had been abandoned shortly after birth and adopted by a wealthy theatre couple Reed and Francis Albee. At the age of thirty he wrote a one act play. The zoo story and presented it himself on his birthday. His writings made him won various awards like 'Lala D' Annunzio award and also Antohette Perry Award, the New York Drama critics circle.

Award and center circle Award for his first full length play i.e. who's Afraid of virgins wolf? (1962). The title of the play was taken from a graffito Screwled on the men's room well. It also stands for reality. The play is an attack on the sterility of American Society and the Vacuity of the success myth on which the country has founded itself. It exposes the hollowness that has crept into American life with the substitution of false values for the real values of the past. All the aspects of American Culture, its dream, success myth, individualism, concept of marriage, manhood and womanhood and the problem of childlessness are focused in this play. This is a story of George (46) and Martha (52) who are returning late at night from a party, thrown by Martha's father. Both are drunks. Marths has also invited a young couple Nick and Honey at this late hour. But after inviting them Gerage and Martha themselves are engaged in making taunts to each other. Martha taunts George for his professional and sexual failures, white George replies her back by singing "Who's afraid of virginis Woolf"?

In their quarrel by chance they reveal the secret of their imaginary child a son. Finally George hits martha's bride by debts the illusion they had .... themselves. But at the end after destroying their illusionary son, they realize the need for each other and begin to think of a new start without creating any fantesy.

A critic described it as a filthy play and criticized it for its morbid and sexual perversity. It was seen as a "persistent escape into morbid fantasy". But later.

It came to be recognized as an example of American theatre's "new maturity" as Robert W. Corrigan describes it.

(3) The setting of the play is a college campus in New Carthege. The name of the campus as New Carthege is very significant which not only provides the setting but also the symbol of its social theme. It presents the New Modern World and the falsity of its values.

(4) His other plays are Ballad of the Sad Cafe (1963) Malcolm (1905) Everything in the Garden 1907) All over (1971), Seascape (1975), pulitzer prize winner listening. (1977) and so many.

Sylvia Plath

Sylvia Plath was born on 27 October 1932, at Massachusetts Memorial Hospital in Boston, Massachusetts. Her parents were Otto Emil Ploth and Aurdia Schober Plath, and brother warsen. After his brother's birth, the family shifted to Johson Avenue in winthrop. This is where Plath became familiar and intimate with the sea. From an early age she enjoyed the sea and could recognize its beauty and power. Her father, a professor of Biology at Boston University and author of a respected treatise on humble bees, died when she was eight. She published her first poem when she was eight. By the time she entered Smith College on a Scholarship in 1950 she already had an impressive list of publications and while at Smith she wrote over four hundred poems.

Plath was awarded a scholarship to Smith college where she wrote fiction and prize winning poetry. Later that summer, she became very depressed and attempted suicide. After receiving extensive Psychiatric treatment as well as shock theropy. She returned to Smith and graduated Summa cum laude in 1955. She was then awarded a fellowship where she met Ted Hughas, also a poet, in February 1956 and married him. She gave birth to her first child in 1960. She continued to write and then gave birth to her second child in 1962.

Sylvia was an accomplished writer, wife and mother, She even described herself as a "triple-threat woman" Friends describe her as energetic, efficient and cheerful and after express surprise or are shocked by the isolation confusion, pain and anger in the colossus (1960), Ariel (1965), Crossing the water (1970, winter trees (1972) her volumes of poetry.

Sylvia Plath is usually assigned the epithet of a confessional poet and that view is facilitated by an apparent autobiographical element in her work. Her poetry has been called confessional and personal and has often been placed in the school of Robert Lowell and anne Sexton. The timeless excellence of her poetry lies in the sense of language and of metaphor. She was a brilliant and compelling lyric poet particularly in the poems of Ariel, which even now, almost 43 years after her suicide, size the reader with their immediate power. Sexton says :

"Poems left behind were technique lasting, but actually over. We talked death and this was life for us, lasting in spite of us, or better, because of us...."

Sylvia Plath has extraordinary powers of correctness accuracy, precision and the power of the visual. John Frederich praises her for the use of English meter and Righting. She uses the rhythm as the life blood of poetry. Ryhtms in her poetry comes from other devices like alliteration, internal rhymes and emphasis on a particular word or group of words like in a poem :

"I am, I am, I am"
The Dead bell
The Dead bell
Death and co." (collected poems)

The technique and style of the poems in The colossus shaws her great craftsmanship. A wide and inventive vocabulary gives insight to the exploration of ideas and feelings. She is also very brilliant at metaphor. But we find some obscurity in her poetry due do references to private history. Like Ariel was the name of her own harse and the meaning of Ariel became clear in Ted Highes' explanatory note.

Thus we can say that Sylvia Plath was one of first American writers to refuse to conceal or disguise her true emotions; in articulating her aggression, hostility and despair in her art, She effectively challenged the traditional literary prioritization of female experience. She was a pioneer and pathfinder .... A Alvarez in his memoir of Sylvia Plath argues that she was by nature a risk taker and that her suicide was her last gamble when she was thirty one year old, which caused the "Jet blood" of poetry to stop forever.

Wallace Stevens

Wallace Stevens, an American Modernist poet was born in Reading, Pennsylvania on October 2, 1879 and died at the age of seventy six in Hartford. All his life stevens collected art from abroad and saw that packages of various government foods were mailed to him regularly. He became interesting in verse-writing at Harvard. Submitting material to the Harvard Advocate. His first work was published in 1915. His first book Harmonium was published in 1923 by the distinguished firm of Alfred A. Knopl. Though he was always much admired by his contemporaries. He added eight new poems in second edition of Harmonium, published in 1931. When Stevens began to write poems with renewed fluency he arranged for them to be printed in limited editions at the same time. His famous works are 1. Ideas of order (1935), Owl's Clover (1937). The Man with the Blue Guitar (1937), parts of a world (1942), Notes toward a Supreme Fiction (1942).

His best known poems include 'Ancedote of the jar, Disillusionment of Ten o'clock, The Emperor of Ice-cream. The Idea of Order at Key West, Sunday Morning, Thirteen ways of looking at a Blackbird.

Stevens, whose work was meditative and philosophical is very much a poet of ideas concerning the relation between consciousness and the world, in Stevens's work 'imagination is not equivalent to consciousness nor is reality equivalent to the world as it exists outside our minds. Reality is the product of the imagination as it shapes the world. Because it is constantly changing as we attempt to find imaginatively satisfying ways to perceive the world, reality is an activity, not a static object.

Stevens suggests that we live in the tension between the shapes we takes the world acts upon us and the ideas of order that our imagination imposes upon the world. The world influences us in our most normal activities. Stevens says that God is a human creation but the feeling of rightness which for so long a time existed with the idea of God may be accessed again. This supreme fiction will be something equally central to our being but contemporary to our lives, in a way that God can never again be. Stevens often write directly about poetry and its human function. Stevens remained a famous poet throughout his age.

James Langston Hughes

James Langston Hughes was a black, who taught the black people, who had lost the ray of hope to live life with dignity and respect. He was the voice of the Black. He was a spokesman for the plight of many black people in America. Langston Highes as an eloquent articulator of anguish, humiliation and anger of African American Community, on account of racial oppression in the U.S. has won him recognization from the critics. He has been hailed as the poet laureate of the African American people.

Hughes was born in Joplin, Missouri, but lived with his grandmother in Lawrence, Kansas, until he was thirteen and then with his mother in Lincoln, where he wrote his first verse. He spent most of his adult life in Herlem. After graduating he planned to visit his father in Mexico and while travelling by train to Mexico, he wrote the most famous poem. The Negro Speaks of River and it appeared in Brownie's book. Later his poems, essays, and short stories appeared in the Brug NAACP Publication Crisis Magazine and in opportunity Magazines one of hughes finest essays appeared in the nation in 1926, entitled "The Negro Artist and the Racial Mountain. It spoke of Black writers and poets, "who would surrender racial pride in the name of a false integration", where a talented Black writer would prefer to be considered a poet, not a black poet. But Hughes argued, "no great poet has ever been afraid of being himself he wrote in his essay :

"We younger Negro artists now intend to express our

individual dark skinned selves without fear or shame. If white people are pleased we are glad. If they aren't, it doesn't matter. We know we are beautiful. And ugly too."

His poetry has been divided into three phases, which is marked by simplicity and directness bespeaking of complete identification with the people whose experience he is recording. Much of his poetry is influenced by his personal life. Because from the very childhood days he has suffered a lot with the feelings of rejection, ignorance and unwanted. He has grown up in a broken family which causes him to grow up very insecure and insure of himself. He suffered a lot because of his skin colour. So his poetry is a reflection of poverty, hardships, racism, inequality etc. of the African American people. He believed that African American are caval to whites. They also have rigit of equality, dignity freedom and opportunity. He presents the world of his people in its positivity, underscores their strength and ability to survive. He always tries to regain the buried identity which his people had brought with them from Africa and which was never completely lost or destroyed.

His poetry was reflection of the African American culture and Harlem. He loved Harlem that was his home. He continued to write even after the Harlem Rehaissence. Actually Harlem Renaissance brought about many great changes. Many things came about during this period like Juzz and blues, poetry, dance and musical theatre. The African-American way of life became the thing. And the credit for the recognization of Black critiers during that period goes to Langston Hughes. In his poetry he shows that his self has splintered or shattered because Americans don't accept them as a part of America. In his famous poem The Negro speaks of River, he feels himself aparted from the land of what they are an important part from the time of evolution. He tries to convince that they have been around as long as rivers. Through this poem he wants the Americans to realize this fact that we are also a part of ancient African civilization of America. He says :

"I've known rivers
I've known rivers as the world and older
than flow of human blood in human vein."

No about hughes has always talked about racism, and about the rights of equality, liberty and freedom. But in order to bring recognization of his own people he never puts down the white race for being prejudiced. He always tries to encourage his own to feel proud of their individuality, of their own heritage, to appreciate their own diversity and culture. He just encourages African Americans to be themselves and to make a foundation fear the future blacks to stand upon so that they can finally be "free within themselves".

Catch 22 by Joseph Heller

Catch 22 is a masterpiece in itself. This is novel which can not be described without using the superlatives. This is the greatest and the funniest novel by Joseph Heller. In his work Heller gives an accurate representation of the madness of war. He has tried his best to open the eyes of the blind world, he started his career as an author of short stories but he got the world wide recognization with the publication of Catch 22. Through this work he satirizes the horross of war and power of powerful bureaucratics to destroy the human spirit. The novel begins as a comic force, leads to the increasingly surreal and then transforms into a nightmarish tragedy. It has a blend of each and every mood. It is a black comedy novel talking about death. The author has given different situations to answer the question that what people do when they face daily likelihood problems. He shows that most of the people try to survive in any way, by hook or by crook.

Catch 22 is a story about Yossarian, a U.S. Army Air Forces B-25 bombardier, and his friends who are stationed with his Air Force sauadronon the island of Pianasa, near the Italian coast in the Mediterranean sea. Yossarian takes this war personally. He tries to avoid the war by getting hospitalized himself because of having a strong desire to live. He feels very troubled and disappointed when he reminds his friends' death in his own arms especially when his saudronon get bombed by its own offices to enhance their own reputation. He expects to get leave to go home but suddenly he gets order that he can't be allowed. It is expected that he will have to go to fly some more missions. He begins to find excuses to prove himself as insane because insanity was the only way to get discharge from duties. Then his officers made his frightened by the name of catch-22. An old woman explains : "Catch 22 says that they have a right to do anything we can't stop them from doing". But Yossarian comes to realize that catch-22 does not actually exist, but this is the way that the bureaucrats are adapting just in order to make others frightened. In the end he finds caged himself in his own dishonest officers hands. He gets a offer that he can either face a court-martial or be released and sent home with honour. There is only one condition; if he wants to be released then he must approve of his officers his support for their policy, which reavires all the men in the Sauadron to fly Eighty missions. But he does not accept the offer of his officer which would cause the death of so many innocent persons and finally gets control of his own life.

Indian Writing in English (Part II)

1. Hyavadan
2. The Autobiography of an Unknown Indian
3. Manohar Malgonkar
4. Geive Petal
5. Chaman Nahal
6. Bhisham Sawhney's Tamas
7. Ghasi Ram Kotwal
8. Train to Pabistan
9. Vibram Seth
10. Shashi Deshpande

Hayavadan

Hayavadan is a famous play written by Girish Karnad, originally in Kannad and later translated in English. Karnad has adapted the play to discuss the problem of identity in a world of tangled relationship. This is a story of two friends Devadatta and Kapila, who are totally different in nature. Davadatta is an intellectual person and a poet. Kapila has a well toned body and feels very energetic everytime. Once devdatta gets attracted towards a girl Padmini and wants to get married. In excitement he even takes an oath that he would give his hands to 'Kali Ma' and his head to 'Lord Rudra', if he fails to get Padmini as a wife. Now Kapila, because of being very attached to his friend, he decides to go to padmini for the proposal of marriage with his friend Devadatta. Finally Devadutta and Padmini get married.

After metting Padmini, Kapila also feels touched, floored and mesmerized by her beauty and nature. He begins to develop a friendly relationship with her and spends more and more time with her. And once Devadatta feels so uncomfortable with their behavior that he gets away himself from them and decides to behead himself in the temple of Kali. When Kapila finds Devadatta's deadbody, he blames himself for that and decides to behead himself. Finally pregnant Padmini goes in search of them and finds their dead bodies. In a fit of shock, she also tries to kill herself but then Goddess kali appears and ask her to attach their heads and she incarnates life in them.

Unfortunately, she mismatches the heads to their bodies

and now the question is who is Padmini's husband. Both claim to be rightful husbands. Then they visit a scholar who speaks in favour of the one who has no Devadatta's head (Kapil's Body) because he thinks that head is the most important organ of our body. The other with Kapila's head and Devadutta's body gets disappointed and escapes into the forest. But soon they feel fed up with their life and decide to kill each other. Now once again the same hands cut the same heads. And Padmini decides to go Sati with their dead bodies.

The Autobiography of an Unknown Indian

The Autobiography of an unknown Indian is an autobiography written by Nirad C. Chaudhari, India's most controversial writer, born at Kishorganj in East Bengal in 23rd November, 1877. He was very much influenced by his family intellectual atmosphere, specially by his father, a lawyer and his mother, an uncompromising puritan. He wrote his first book, The Autobiography of an unknown citizen in 1951, and followed by many others including. The continent of Circe, for which he won the Duff Cooper Memorial Prize. In 1970 he moved to England and in 1992 Queen Elizabeth Li conferred upon him the title of Honorary commander of the british Empire.

IAN JACK has observed that in this book, Chaudhuri is courageous in two ways : in his literary ambition and in the open declaration of his political and historical. He has described his life chapter by chapter, his birth place, his parents, his experiences and adventures. He has tried to make us familiar to the roads of Calcutta, where he spent most of the part of his life. When he began to write this book, he had no ideals before him. He was genuinely an unknown citizen living in Delhi. He says that this is not just a personal Autobiography, but also a biography of Nation.

He has devided the written history of India into three phases in his work. The first phase begins about 500 B.C. to

1192 A.D., the year that India lost its independence to Muslim invaders. The second period may be referred as Dark Ages, for India. The third phase which he refers to as the British period, began about 1774 A.D., When India became a British Colony.

The author says that the Indians were never reconciled with Muslim rule and were never prepared to accept it. But when British overthrew Muslim rule, India became part of the Western world. The Hindus accepted the new values, the Muslims, on the other hand, did not accept the British rule and the resulting loss of political power. Chaudhri says that Hindu society is essentially a close society, based on birth and blood ties. The presence of certain Islamic elements in Hindu society was an external imposition only.

Thus Chaudhuri's power as a describer speaks for itself in the pages that follow and needs no elaboration, he is fascinating, ground-level witness and expositor of a vanished Indian way of life and of what British imperialism.

Manohar Malgonkar

Manohar Malgonkar born on 12 July 1913 is a prominent Indo-Anglian novelist who made a distinct contribution to the literary world. He is well known for his novels and short fiction. He also worked as an officer in the Maratha light infantry, a big game hunter, a civil servant, a mine owner and a farmer. He also took interest in politics and stood for parliament. He did graduation with honours in English and Sanskrit from Bombay University because of having a royal background. He used to give the public lectures also because of having command over English language. His spoken sentences are as precise and rounded as those he writes. He talks very quickly, confidently, and eagarly. After serving Army for some time to the rank of Lieutenant-Colonal he turned himself to business and farming.

Malgonkar is not only a novelist but also a historian having written three books on Indian History. Kanhoji Angrey (1959) Puors of Dewas Senior (1902) and Chhatrapatis of Kolhapur (1971)

He has also written various scripts for Indian movies, short stories and more than hundreds of articles. His famous novels are *Distant Drums, Combat of Shadows The princess, A bend in the Ganges* and *The Devil's Wind.*

Distant Drum is a story of two friends Kiran and Abdul, who are hostile to each other, after the partition in 1947, since one is Hindu and the other is Muslim, one is assigned to Indian army and other to Pakistan Army. He has described very beautifully, how did they meet at the border?

It is symbolic presentation of the Indian encounter with the British Army and its value for India. Combat of shadows shows the problems of the labourers of tea plantation of Assam in a very realistic way. All his major novels and short stories taken together reveal him a writer keenly interested in Indian social life. Through his novels he has always shown the psychological and the sociological factors that form the basis of human relationships.

Thus Manohar Malgonhar has a special branch for close introspection of the Indian sociopolitical complexity in historical perspectives. He becomes vocal even on those topics which discreet writers generally avoid. He does not have the fascination to articulate the National Movement romantically nor does he spare the followers of the Father of Nation, Mahatma Gandhi. He is always remembered for his animated, persuasive and competent style. His novels have contrived plots, dynamic language, readability, mature thoughts and suspenseful presentation.

Geive Patel

Geive Patel born in Mumbai in 1940, is a self taught artist, a poet and a playwright. He also practised to be a general physician. He has achieved the world wide recognization specially in poetry. He has been conducing a poetry workshop in Rishi Valley School for over a decade. He has participated in many exhibitions as well as organized his own. In 1966, he held his first show in Mumbai and went to organize various exhibitions in India and abroad. He has portrayed Two Men with hand cart, Fishers, The Water Tank at Nargal, very beautifully on the Canvas. He has also exhibited for contemporary Indian Art gallary, New York, 1981, and 'Coups de Cover' Geneva, 1987. Among his poems, On Killing Tree is the best, in which Patel has personified a tree and has shown the expressions and instructions on the correct way to extract the tree from the earth. The poem tells us as a hidden meaning that Mother Nature is evitable and can not be destroyed. If you want to cut tree, it is not an easy job, it will take a long time. By cutting stems and branches, the tree can not be cut. It is through the root that we can cut it, but it is also a long process. In the same way human life is not so easy to end. For his unique poetry and mastery over Canvas, he has also been awarded by woodrow wilson fellowship, washington DC 1984 and Rockefeller fellowship, University of Chicago, 1992. His other famous works are like Bombay Central Forensic Medicine, God or, Old Man's Death, Post Mortem and So on. In his Introduction, Give Patel talks about his poetry and the workshops in which he gives an understanding of how the nebulous space of the poetic imagination can be taught in a structured manner. He has really structured his workshop but he also kept it flexible. It is this flexibility that allowed the young people to move from an attitude of suspicion to engagement and explore their own poetic instincts very effectively.

In an interview, Patel describes himself as "a profane monk" whose poetry reveals "a slightly sick concern with the body". Sudesh Mishra writes that Give Patel belongs to the same generation as Jussawalls and Mehrotra, he is a poet whose vision elades simplistic modernist labels and equations.

Chaman Nahal

Chaman Nahal born in Sialkot (Pakistan) in 1927 was honoured by Sahitya Academy award in 1977, and Federation of Indian Publishers award, 1977, 1979 because of being the best novelist. Nahal's distinction lies in writing about India without any touch of exoticism. He worked as a lecturer at a University in India, 1949-1962. He had also been a visiting lecturer at several universities in the U.S.A., Malaysia, japan, Singapore, Canada and North Korea. Nahal's creative writings seem to be an embodiment of his positive attitude to life—its acceptance in its totality, the celebration of its joys and resignation to its sufferings. The acceptance, affirmation, celebration and exploration of individual life seem to form the heart of Nahal's works. He himself says, "I have largely concerned myself with two themes in my novels, the individuals vs. the joint family system in India and my historical identity as an individual, as an Indian. For the latter theme I have drawn extensively on history, especially our freedom movement 1915-1947. Azadi, *The Crown and the Loincloth* and *The Salt of Life* are part of a quartet on that theme; I'm working on the fourth volume of the quartet now. I use Gandhi as the ultimate symbol of that identity.

Azadi, a Sahitya Academy Award winning novel, tells about the truth regarding partition than any historical study. It is description of the daily lives of seven families, of Hindus and Muslims. The novel shows how did they share their interests, religion, business, attended mixed classes, Joined a mixed police force and army. But finally in 1947, it all disappeared because of partition. The novel ends with a sadly depleted family trying to begin life a new in delhi.

In *The Gown and the Loincloth,* Nahal shows Mahatma Gandhi as a central character. He presents Gandhi directly as well as in terms of effect.

He has on the family of Thakur Shanti Nath, a land owner in a Punjabi family.

The second novel The Salt of life mainly describes about Gandhi's salt Satyagraha of 1930. At present he is an author of 22 books including a novels among them. By portraying India very beautifully in his works Nahal has earned a great appraisal both at home and abroad.

Bhisham Sawhneys Tames

Tamas (Darkness) is written by a famous Hindi writer, playwright, and Padma Bushna awarded actor Bhisham Sahni. Whatever Sahni has witnessed in his Struggle for Indian Independence, he has portrayed everything in this powerful and passionate novel Tamas. Sahni, born on Aug. 915 in Rawal Pindi, earned his education from Lahore and Amritsar. After partition he began to live in Amritsar with his family. He also worked as a stage performer in Mumbai and later joined as a lecturer in English in Delhi College. He translated twenty five books from Russian into Hindi, while doing his job as a translator. He himself performed in his film Tamas, Aparna Sen's Mr. and Mrs. Iyer (2002) for which he was awarded Uttar Pradesh Govt. award for Tamas and India's highest literary award the Sahitya Academe fellowship in 2002.

Tamas is a story of, true events of riots of partition in 1947. Most of the character are with their real names to give a touch of reality to the novel. The novel begins with the scene, when Nathu accepts the proposal to kill a pig. After some time the pig occurs on a mosque steps. And now Muslims revolts and takes the revenge by killing a cow. Sahni has portrayed all those experiences in the form of Tamas. There are so many chilling consequences is the novel, like we feel touched when a young kid kills an old man, and the other is where many sikh women drown themselves into a well just for the sake of self defence from the Rioters.

Sahni has very beautifully portrayed the political

atmosphere of that time. In fact he reminds that politicians are the first step towards the insanity of human kind. He showed how the Britishers got success in implementing their devide and rule policy. All the incidents are woven so fantastically that makes the novel almost an episode by epidote drama.

Ghasiram Kotwal

Ghasiram Kotwal is a world wide recognized play in English translation from original Marathi. It was a creation by Vijay Tendular, who wrote his first story at the age of six and directed at ėleven. Born in 1928, Tendular started his professional career as a journalist, public relation officer and finally as a prolific writer. He has written twenty eight plays, seven collections of one act plays, children's plays, short stories, three essays and more than seventeen film scripts. He has been honoured by a number of awards like Maharashtra State government reward, Sangeet Natak academy award, the film fare Award, Padambhushan, and the life time achievement award of Katha Chudamani Award in 2001. He got the appraisal, specially for Ghasiram Kotwal, Gidhade, Court Chalu Ahe, Kamala, Kanyadan and his movie Aakrosh, Manthan, Ardha Satya for portraying the social issues of the era.

Ghasiram Kotwal is the story of Maharashtra state in the late eighteenth century. Tendulkar has portrayed the picture of politics and the political powers. It is a strong political satire and shows how the men in powers use others to fulfill their own purpose and then destroy them when they become useless. This is a story about Nana Phadnavis, one of corrupt ministers in the court of the Peswa of Pune, and Ghasiram, who is a Brahmin and Charged with theft and got imprisoned. Here his friendship starts with Nana and his revenge with the people of Pune. With the help of Nana, Ghasiram's daughter gets posted as a Kotwal and

Ghasiram begins to take revenge by putting the people in jail even for very small offence. But at the same time Nana is using his daughter for his physical need, and as a result while giving birth to a baby she gets died.

Once again Ghasiram feels frustrated but now because of Nana, whom he was thinking as his friend. In the end after getting complaint from the Brahmins, Nana orders Ghasiram to be killed.

The play was also adapted into a film Ghasiram Kotwal (1976), in which Om Puri performed as an actor.

Train to Pakistan (1956)
Kushwant Singh

Khuswant Singh (1915) is an eminent editor, historian. Journalist, short story writer and a novelist. He writes articles, reviews for the newspapers. He has written a few stories and a couple of Novels. His famous novels are Train to Pakistan (1956) and I Shall Not Hear the Nightingale (1959). A movie based on the novel Train To Pakistan (1998) was released. It was nominated in cinequest Son. Jose festival. India got freedom on 15 August, 1947 but the nation's triumph was marred by the sectarian violence which attended the partition of the sub-continent. In 'Train to Pakistan', Khushwant Singh recounts the tragedy as it befalls mano majra, a tiny village close to the frontier between India and Pakistan. The Sikhs are so sensible that they inform everything that happens and this is their style of living. The narrative moves on two levels, first, a realistic account of the rising tensions and hostilities among the Sikh and Muslim Villagers. Who until that moment, have lived peacefully together.

Second, a symbolic shadowing forth, through images of the river choked with dead bodies and the silent trains packed with carnage of a unspeakable horror of the catastrophe with all its madness and ferocity making it all the more convincing and devastating. Its varied and strongly individualized characters, its sense of place and ethos, its feeling for the spirit and style of the Sikhs are the products of resourceful imaginative strength capable of imparting life to character and drama plot.

Upon learning that the government was planning to transport Muslims from Mano Majra to Pakistan the next day for their safety. After the Muslims leave to a refugee camp from where they will eventually go to Pakistan, a group of religious agitators come to Mano Majra and instills in the local Sikhs a hatred for Muslims and convince a local gang to attempt mass murder as the Muslims leave on their train to Pakistan.

Khushwant Singh does not describe the politics of the partition in detail. This is mostly because his purpose is to bring out the individual, human element and provide a social understanding, two aspects of historical events which tend to be either ignored or not covered effectively in texts. Singh makes it clear that many people played a part in this chaos and everyone was equally worthy of blame, all while integraing examples of the sheer moral confusion which arises from trying to make sense of an event as momentuous as the partition.

Vikram Seth (1952)

Vikram Seth is a well known India poet, novelist and travel writer. He has studied several languages like Welsh, German, French, Urdu etc. His family lived in many cities including the Bata Shoe Company town of Batanagar amal, Patna and London. His father was an executive with the Bata India Limited shoe company and his mother was the first woman judge on the Delhi High Court and the first woman chief justice of a state high court, at Shimla. Seth has been awarded with many prizes and wards. He has got Padma Shri in Literature and Education in 2007.

His Volume of poetry are 1. Mappings (1980), 2. The Humble Administrator's Garden (1985), All you who sleep Tonight (1990). He has published from Heaven Lake. Travels Through Sinkiang and Tibet. But he is best known for his epic novel A Suitable Boy (1993) and his verse novel The Golden Gate (1986).

The Golden Gate is a witty novel. It is written in a form of sonnet borrowed from Pushkin's Eugene Onegin. It portrays the life style of California through the story of the relationships of a group of young professionals.

An Equal Music (1999) is a love story about a Violinist. He pursues the lady he loved in his youth but he remains surprised on being find her deaf and married. Vikram Seth explores the World of professional quartet. Seth also writes well about music.

A Suitable Boy (1993) is a long epic novel about the Mehras' search for a suitable husband for a daughter, Lata.

Lata and her mother have different ideas on What Constitutes a suitable boy for Lata to marry. The novel is set in post-independence India. It concerns four families, the Mehras, the Kapoors, the Chatterjis (Hindu) and the Khans (Muslim). The novel tries to re-imagine the nation. There is light social comedy, detailed political analysis and romance.

Vikram Seth uses visual detail in a unique style in an attempt to convey a sense of the meaning underlying everyday behaviour and objects. His works evoke the atmosphere, society and landscapes of India.

Shashi Deshpande

Shashi Deshpande born in 1938 in Dharward, Karnatka, India was a daughter of a famous Sanskrit scholar and renowned Kannada dramatist Sriranga. She received degrees in Economics and Law and was a gold medalist. She is a prolific writer and has published nine novels and seven story collections. She is a major contemporary Indian woman writer, whose fiction can be read as a manual to understand how the tendered identity in Indian Society comes into being. In her works and interviews she has uncovered the boundaries created around a woman's life from childhood to womanhood in the traditional male-dominated Indian Society. She always tries to show through her works that how the traditional norms of our Indian Society mould women's inner life and encourages them to put up with the insensitivity of the male ethos. Her woman characters are very much conscious of their marginalized position in the male dominated society and want to achieve their individuality. In her first novel *The Dark Holds No Terror* (1980) she shows how the independence of girls, is corbed by the social norms of male dominated society. Whatever the liberty is given to a boy is denied to a girl. Even the birth of a daughter is considered as a misery. The girls are just encouraged by the society to play their roles of daughter, wife and mother. They are not supposed to do anything more constructive, creative than men. Like In *The Dark Hold No Terrors,* When Saru, a doctor, begins to earn more than her husband, it arises many problems in their relationship. In her another novel *Roots and Shadows* (1983), She shows how the mothers want to mould their daughters into better women, who can fulfill the needs of their men, instead of better human beings with their own individuality. Indu, the protagonist of the novel, who is an educated and working woman once says, "I had sobbed out my heart to old uncle one day. And he had said, "For a woman, intelligence is always a burden, Indu, we like our women not to think."

She received the Sahitya Academy Award and Nanjangud Thrirumelamba award for her fabulous work in the novel *That Long Silence.* She has been actively involved in writing books for children. She is a well known name in the field of Indian Literature and a award winning novelist. Today she is a recognized Indian Voice.

Course XIX (Option I)
Colonical and Past Colonial Studies
(Part II)

1. Homi Bhabha on Hybridity
2. Nadine Gordimer
3. Orientalism
4. Ben Okar's A Way of Being Free
5. Ania Roomba's Colonialism/Post Colonialism
6. V.S. Naipaul's A Bend in the River
7. Spivak's Can the Subaltern speak?
8. Evelyn Waugh's Black Mischief
9. Kazuo Ishiqaro's The Remains of the Day
10. Francis Fukuyama's The End of History and the Last Man

Homi Bhabha Hybridity

Hybridity originates from the latin hybrida, A hybrid is something that is mixed, and hybridity is simply mixture. It is the productivity of colonial power shifting its forces and fixities.

Bhabha like many post colonial and post modern theorists, argue that hybridity, as an expression of ambivalence and fluidity, represents an active moment of challenge and resistance against a dominate cultural power. According to Bhabha, hybridity the potential to intervene and dislocate the process of colonization through the reinterpretation of political discourse. Bhabha himself says that I have developed the concept of hybridity to describe the construction of cultural authority within conditions of political antagonism or in equity. Hybrid agencies find their voice in a dialectic that does not seek cultural supremacy or sovereign. It is within the third space of the hybrid that culture as art, culture-as-narrative, emerges as visions of community" and 'versions of historic memory' what the hybrid does is to make both colonizer and colonized aware that culture can not be mummified. Culture is alive, as seen in the hybrid, which Bhabha calls, "the contaminated get connective tissue between cultures Bhabha continues that within the Third Space of the interstice, colonizer and colonized negotiate their cultural difference and create a culture that is a hybrid, which "is the revolution of the assumption of colonial identity of both colonizer and colonized. So in a sense, their negotiation is dialectic, but a dialectic that remains ambivalent.

According to Bhabha, In betweeness is the reality of cultural mix when one is drawing from many cultures in a structural context. And hybridity is cultural result of that mix. So we can say that the word hybridity sounds like a way to describe the interdependent relationship between the colonized and the colonizer leading to some kind of hybrid culture which has taken a part of each.

According to Toni Morrison Homi Bhabha is one of that small group occupying the front ranks of literary and cultural theoretical thought. Any serious discursion on Post Colonial, post modern scholarship is inconceivable without referring Mr. Bhabha Mr. Edward said about Bhabha that he is a rare thing, a reader of chormous subtety and wit, a theorist of uncommon power. His work is a landmark in the exchange between age genres and cultures, the colonial post colonial, modernist and postmodern. In his best work The Location of Culture, Bhabha uses concepts such as mimicry, interstice, hybridity and liminality to argue that cultural production is always most productive where it is most ambivalent.

Nadine Gordimer

Nadine Gordimer, born in 1923 and in seamus Hearney's words, one of "the Guerrilles of the imagination "because the first South African and the seventh woman to be awarded the Nobel Prize for Literature in 1991. Over half a century Gordimer has written thirteen novels, over two hundred short stories and several volumes of essays. Ten books are devoted to her work and about two hundred critical essays appear in her bibliography. In 1959, she published *A World of Strangers.* In her third novel occasion for Loving (1963) she deals with the failure of tolerance and humanism, the increasing absurdity of the race laws brought friendship and love across the colour bar to a halt. In the fourth novel The Late Bourgeois World (1966), the choice is between the naive idealism of Saboteurs or the well meaning cynimism of passive liberals. In 1971, she published A Guest of Honour, which describes the birth pays of new Africa. Her Booker Prize Winner novel The Conservationist evokes the sterility of the white community. This novel is full of ironies.

In her novels, Gordimer reveals the situations when reality suddenly takes another course and we are caught in our roles and expectations, in the traps of skin colour, class, family and the body itself. The most famous of her work is A Sport of Nature, In which she has shown her affection for blacks. She has always dealt with love and politics. In her novels, she has always shown her interest towards the search for an identity, a self confrontation, and a wish to belong and exist. Her characters are always living in the shadow of violence, threatened by unpredictable brutality. She works in the imaginative dimension, always on an expedition into the mysteries of human experience.

In her collection of short stories, Face to Face, she has described the psychological consequences of a racially divided society. Her novel the lying days is based on her own life and has portrayed a girl named, Helen, and has shown her growing disaffection toward the narrow mindlessness of a small town life. She was a founding member of Congress of South African writers, and even at is apartheid height, she never considered going into exile. She was very active in the anti-apartheid movement, joining the African National Congress during the days when the organization was banned. She has also participated actively to find out HIV/AIDS Causes.

Orientalism

Orientalism is primarily a term used for the imitation or depiction of aspects of Eastern cultures in the West by writers, designers and artists. The 20th century Scholar Edward said in his controversial book orientalism, uses the term to describe a pervassive western tradition, both academic and artistic, of prejudiced outsider interpretations of the East, shaped by the attitudes of European imperialism in the 18th and 19th centuries. The orientalism refers to orient and the orient means 'The East'. It is a book written by Edward said, In this book said has described, "My contention is that orientalism is fundamentally a political doctrine willed over the orient because the orient was weaker than the West, which elided the orient's difference with its weaknesses.... As a cultural apparatus orientalism is all aggression, activity, judgement, will-to-truth and knowledge" (orientalism, P.204) Said suggests that all cultures have a view of other cultures that may be exotic and harmless to some extent, but it is not this view that he argues against and when this view is taken by a militarily and economically dominant culture against another it can lead to disastrous results. He suggests that this orientalist discourse was set up as a foundation for all further study. He states that : The four elements I have described-expansion, historical confrontation, sympathy, classification are the currents in 18th century thought on whose presence the specific intellectual and institutional structures of modern orientalism depend". He describes only in this book how does one represent other culture? What is another culture? Is the notion of a different culture a useful one or does it always get involved either in self-congratulations or hostility and aggression.

(orientalism, P.325)

In short orientalism is cited as a detailed work within the study of orientalism and is considered to be Edward said's most influential work and has been translated into more than 36 languages. His evaluation and critique of the set of beliefs known as orientalism forms an important background for postcolonial studies. Said states that by orientalism I mean several things, all of them, are interdependent. The most readily accepted designation for orientalism is and academic one orientalism is a style of thought. Thus a number of courtiers have accepted the basic distinction between the East and the West.

Ben Okri's A way of Being tree

Winner of Booker Prize for fiction, Ben Okri was born in 1959 in Minna Northern Nigeria. As the witness of civil war in Nigeria, much of his early fiction gives a reflection of political violence. He is not only a novelist but also a poet. His collection of poems, An African Elegy was published in 1992 and an epic poem, Mental Flight, in 1999. His most famous A collection of essays, A Way of being Free, was published in 1997. In some of his books, he has also tried to bring together the poetry and the story.

A way of being Free confirms Ben Okri's status as one of the most inspiring of contemporary writers. He has presented the essays in apart form in this collection. He has included the various range from the personnel to the analytical including the meditation on the role of the poet. The book can be seen as a call to the poets of the poet and those who have forgotten how to be poets. Okri speaks of engaging actively with the world, of constant questioning, of fighting for and studying up for our dreams. Through this book, the author reminds us about the beauty of life and encourages us to live with full passion. He helps us to recharge our psyche and shake cobwebs off spirit. He says that there are no says without mountains having been climbed. The joys that spring from the challenges are profound, and the challenges will always be there. As long as there are human beings there are challenges.

Okri believes that there are many ways to die and not all of them have to do with extinction. A lot of them have to do with living. Living many lies. Living without asking questions living in the cave of your own prejudices. Living the life imposed on you, the dreams and codes of your ancestor. Once Okri quoted that "we plan our lives according to a dream that came to us in our childhood, and we find that life alters our plans.

Because of having such type of views about life, Okri has also been described as a magic realist. His first hand experiences of civil war in Nigeria all said to have inspired many of his works. He writes about both the mundane and the metaphysical, the individual and the collective, drawing the reader into a world with vivid descriptions.

Ania Loomba's Colonialism and Post Colonialism

Ania Loomba is the Katherine Bryson Professor at the University of Pennsylvania. She is the author of Colonialism/Post Colonialism, Race and Colonialism and Renaissance Draw, as well as the co-editor of postcolonial studies. She examins the key features of the ideologies and history of colonialism, the relationship of Colonial discourse to literature, challenges to Colonialism and recent developments in post Colonial theories and histories in the writings of contemporary theorist including Edward said, Homi Bhabha and Spivak. Ania Loomba is very ideal for her purpose. She writes with clarity, patiently explains, provides summaries of contrary opinion and shows how the topics that have become the part of postcolonial studies have their origin, method or insights in other area such as feminism, Marrism, Structuralism, post structuralism and psychuanalyses. She points out in her book, "Grams is argued that the ruling classes achieve domination not by force or coercion alone, but also by creating subjects who "willingly" submit to being "ruled". Every human being in addition to bring their own personal identity, has a sense of who they are in relation to the large community the nation. Postcolonial studies is an attempt to strip away conventional perspective and examine what that national identity might be for a post colonial subject.

She states, "Perhaps the connection between

postcolonial writing and the nation can be better comprehended by understanding that the 'nation' itself is a ground of dispute and debate, site for the competing imagining of different ideological and political interests. Basically colonialism is a practice of domination which involves the subjugation of one people to another.

And Post Colonialism is a specifically post modern intellectual discourse that holds together a set of theories found among the texts and sub texts of philosophy, film, political science, human geography and literature. These theories are reactions to the cultural legacy of colonialism. It deals with cultural identity in colonized societies : the dilemma of developing a national identity after Colonial rule Looma all looks at how sexuality is figured in the text of Colonialism and how contemporary feminist ideas and concept intersect with those of post-Colonialist thought.

Colonialism can be defined as the conquest and control of other people land and goods. But Colonialism in this sense is not merely the expansion of various European powers into Aria, Africa, or Americans from the Sixteenth century onwards, it has been a recurrent and widespread feature of human history.

A BEND IN THE RIVER.
V.S.Nai Paul

A Bend in the River (1979) is a great novel written by V.S. Naipaul. It was short listed for the Booker Prize in 1979 V.S. Naipaul was awarded Nobel Prize for literature in 2001. Vidiadhar Surajprasad Naipaul (1932) is a British novelist and essayist of Indo-Trinidadian descent.

The novel is set in an unnamed African Country after independence. The story of the novel is narrated by an Indian Muslim boy, Salim, who is a shopkeeper in a small city. He never identifies the country where he lives. But he observes the rapid changes in his homeland with an outsider's distance. The need of the individual to know the history of society in order to understand the present can never be underestimated. The timeless & river and the bush are part of Africa's part and history. The displacement as a theme serves as a device to narrate the events from an outsider's viewpoint against the backdrop of post colonial failure. Salim suggests : All that had happened in the past was washed away : there was only the present. It was as though, as a result of some disturbance in the heavens the early morning light was always reading into the darkness and men lived in a perpetual down." Inder, Salim's childhood friend and compariot from the east coast of Africa functions as a kind of alter ego for Salim while other characters as foil for the narrator. Inder is a failure of imagination and proper perspective.

Salim is an admirer of Nazruddin. He considers him as his family friend and adopts him as his model even more for his European manners rather than his money, philosophy or strategies of business skills. Salim tries to find his post in a union with the daughter of Nazruddin. One cannot live for ever "in a free state" without identity, direction of hope. The novelist's only need is for some kind of faith which Salim wants to have. Salim doubts whether he would be able to make himself accordingly to ideas or the possibilities he has.

The world is what it is and nothing else. The much quoted full sentence, the opening statement of A Bend in the River reads : "The world is what it is men and nothing, who allow themselves to become nothing, have no place in it." This is an epigram for Naipaul's existential social philosophy. The writer as an interpreter presents us with an imaginative reconstruct of history, giving telling details and a factual portrayal of events.

Spivak's can the Subaltern Speak?

Gayatri Chakravorty Spivak (born Feb. 24, 1942) is an Indian literary critic and theorist. She gained the world wide recognization after the publication of her article 'Can the Subaltern Speak?" She earned her Ph.D. degree from University of lowa. She also earned popularity because of her subsequent translation of Derrida's "Of Grammatology". She has often referred to herself as a "Practical Marxist-feminist-deconstructionist. Subaltern is a term that commonly refers to persons who are socially, politically and geographically outside of the hegemonic power structure. The term is used in postcolonial theory. Some thinkers use it in a general sense to refer to marginalize groups and the lower classes. But Gayatri Chakravorty Spivak use it as a more specific sense. She argues that "Subaltern is not just a clarry word for oppressed, for other, for somebody who's not getting piece of pie. They are within the hegemonic discourse wanting a piece of the pie and not being allowed so let them speak, use the hegemonic discourse. They should not call themselves subaltern." Spivak carriers on several struggles simultaneously the first and the most important is her intervention in the debates surrounding the field of subaltern. In particular, she objects to notion that Subaltern studies seeks to allow the previously ignored voice of the subaltern finally to be heard and that its objective can be to "establish true knowledge of the subaltern and consciousness." In this essay she shows in contrast that "Derrida is less dangerous" than Foucault, who not only privileges "the concrete' 'Subject of oppression,', but even more dangerously conceals the privilege, he thus grants himself by 'masauerading as the absent non-represented who lets the oppressed speak for themselves." Spivak proposes the antidote of a single question : can the subaltern speak? It is a testimony to the power of Spivak's essay that this question has come to dominate the entire theoretical field to such an extent the Vast majority of responses have consisted of answer to, rather than examinations of, her question.

In her essay, Spivak encourages group, a project led by Ranjit Guha that has reappropriated Gramsci's teen "Subaltern" in order to locate and re-establish a "Voice" or collective locus of agency in post colonial India. Although she acknowledges the "epistemic violence" done upon Indian subalterns.

Evelyn Waugh's Black Mischief

Evelyn Waugh was born in London in a middle class family. He was more attached to his mother as compare to his father. He was educated at Lancing College, Sussex and at Hereford College, Oxford, Where he read Modern history. During his college days, he was not treated well by his upper-class classmates. Because of this disappointment he spent his college years in drinking. Once he also tried to commit suicide. But later he used all his experiences in his writings and gained a world wide recognization. Now he is regarded by many as the leading satirical novelist of his day. He established his literary reputation with the novel *Decline and Fall,* an episodic story of Paul Penny feather who is expelled from oxford.

Black mischief tells the story of the fictional state of Azania—an island of the east coast of Africa. Its new ruler, the English educated Seth (the chief of the chiefs of Sabuyu) is determined to drag his empire into the modern age. For this he likes help of his oxford acquainstance Basil seal who makes plans for constitutional reform and a distrous birth control etc. In Black Mischief, Emperor Seth resorts "to the power of advertisement" in order to teach his illiterate Azanian subjects "the benefits of birth control", he circulates "a large, highly coloured poster that portrayed two contrasted scenes. On one side a native hut overrun with children of every age suffering from physical incapacity and on the other side a bright parlor furnished with chairs and table, the mother, beautiful and healthy father and the single child. The pictures include the world; which home do you choose? It was his goal to 'modernise his country, But at a 'Birth Control Parade" organized by Seth, Ballon and several religious leaders overthrow the Emperor and install and install his senile uncle Achon. However, Achon dies upon coronation, and Seth dies in hiding. With no heir to the monarchy, the league of Nations steps in and claims the country as a league of Nations Mandate.

Kajuo Ishiguros the Kemains to the Day

The booker prize winner for the best fiction in 1989, *The Remains of the Day* is one of the most highly regarded post war British novels written by Japanese British author Kazuo Ishiguro. After the publication of his first novel, Kazuo Ishiguro was nominated by Granta magazine as one of the 20 'Best of the young British writers' He was also included in the same promotion when it was repeated in 1993.

The Remain of the Day is Ishiguro's third novel and is set in the post war England. It tells the story of an elderly English butler confronting disillusionment as he recalls a life spent in service, memories viewed against a backdrop of war and the rise of Fascism. The title of the novel refers to evening, when a person can reflect on a day's work. Evening here is a symbol for old age, when one can look back and access one's life work. It also suggest what is left after a wreck.

Like Ishiguro's other novels, the story is told from the first person point of view with the narrator recalling his life through a letter to an unknown person, perhaps another butler. It is a story of Stevens, an English butler, who has spent three years in the service of Lord Darlington. The novel begins, when Stevens receives a letter from his ex-colleague called Miss Kenton describing her married life, which seems an unhappy one. As he receives the letter, he looks back to his relationship with miss Kentoa, that he once had. At the same time he gets an opportunity to borrow a car and to go for a trip from his employer, a wealthy American named Mr. Faraday. It shows his loyalty to Lord darlington. So he decides to to go for a five day motoring trip and finally the climax of this journey is to be a reunion with his former housekeeper Miss Kenton. He goes back in his past and thinks about Miss Kenton's feelings for him. He is fully aware of those feelings and fails to reciprocate. It is not only the social situations, but also his emotional maturity (or it may be immaturity) that holds him back. During his service at Darlington Hall, Stevens Chose to maintain a sense of dignity, as opposed to searching and discovering the feelings that existed between himself and Miss Kenton. But they enjoy each other's company. In the end it emerges that, she has been married for over 20 years and therefore is no longer Miss Kenton but has become Mrs. Benn. She also admits what her life with Stevens might have been Stevens muses over lost opportunities and he focuses on the remains of day, referring to his future service with Mr. Farraday.

Francis Fubyam's The Endo of History and the Last Man

Francis Fukuyama born on 27 October 1952, is an American philosopher, political economist and author. He earned his Ph.D. degree in government from Harvard University. He is best known as the author of the End of History and the last Man, He has also written a number of other books like *Trust : the Social virtues and the Creation of prosperity,* which he dedicated to his wife Laura Holmgren, *Our Post human future : Consequences of the Biotechnology Revolution,* The great disruption : Human Nature and the Reconstruction of social order, in which he explores the origin of social norms and other book he published was falling behind : Explaining the development Gap between Latin America and the United States.

The End of History and the Last Man is a book written in 1992, it was just an expansion of an essay "The End of History" published in 1989 in an International Journal The National Interest. The book deals with many aspects of culture, history and political, social and economic Philosophy. But the central thesis is quite simple. In *this book, Fubryame Argued that* The original article that is the end of History excited an extraordinary amount of commentary and controversy, first in the United States and then in a series of countries like England, France, Italy, the Soviet Union, Brazil, Japan etc. People were conferred for the use of a word 'history'. Understanding history in an conventional sense as the occurrence of events, the people pointed to the fall of the Berlin Wall, the Chinese communist crackdown in Tiananmen Square and the Iraqi invasion of Kuwait. But Fubeyama says that what I suggested had come to an end was not the occurrence of events, even large, grave events but History : that is, history understood as a single, coherent, evolutionary process, when taking into account the experience of all people in all times. He believes that history should be viewed as an evolutionary process and he stresses that the events still occur at the end of History. The end of history means liberal democracy will become the only form of government for all states. This form of government will be the last form of government. He argues that "What may be witnessing is not just the end of the cold was, or the passing of a particular period of Post War history, but the end of history as such. That is, the end point of mankind's ideological evolution and universalization of western liberal democracy as the final form of human government". He does not claim at any point that events will stop happening in the future. What he is claiming is that all that will happen in future is that democracy will become more and more prevalent in the long term, although it may have temporary setbacks.

English Language (Part II)

1. Imagery
2. Metaphor
3. Symbolism
4. Euphemism
5. Transformational-Generative Grammar
6. ESP
7. Bilingualism
8. Second Language acquisition
9. Handling of large classes
10. Situational Language Teaching

Imagery

This term is one of the most common in criticism, and one of the most variable in meaning. Its applications range all the way from the 'mental pictures' which, it is sometimes claimed, are experienced by the reader of a poem to the totality of the components which make up a poem. Imagery is used to signify all the objects and qualities of sense perception referred to in a poem or other work of literature, whether by literal description, by allusion or in the vehicles (the secondary references) of its similes and metaphors. In William Wordsworth's "She Dwelt among the Untrodden Ways" (1800), the imagery in this broad sense includes the literal objects the poem refers to (for example,, "untrodden ways," "Springs," "grave") all well as the "Violet" of the metaphor and the star" of the simile in the second stanza. The term Imagery image should not be taken to imply a visual reproduction of the object denoted, some readers of the passage experience visual images and some do not : and among those who do, the explicitness and details of the pictures very greatly.

In his *In Memoriam* (1850) No. 101, for example, Tennyson's imagery encompasses not only things that are visible, but also qualities that are smelled, casted or heard together with a suggestion, in the adjective a summer, "of Warmth'.

Unloved, that beach will gather brown,...
And many a rose-carnation feed
With summer spice the humming air...

Imagery is used more narrowly to signify only specific descriptions of visible objects and scenes, especially if the description is vivid and particularized.

Caroline spurglon, in 'Shakespeare's Imagery and What It tells US (1935), made statistical courts of the reference of the figurative vehicle in Shakespeare, and used the results as clues to Shakespeare's personal experiences, interests and temperament. She also presented evidence that a number of the individual plays have characteristic image motifs (for example, animal imagery in king lear, and the figure of disease, corruption and death in Hamlet); her view was that these elements established the overall atmosphere of a play. Some new critics held that the implicit interactions of the imagery in distinction form explicit statements by the author or the overt speeches and actions of the characters was the way that the controlling literary subject, or theme, worked itself out in many plays, poems and novels.

Metaphor

Donald Davidson in an essay 'What Metaphors Mean" (1978), mounted a challenge to the standard assumption that there is a metaphorical meaning as distinct from a literal meaning. "Metaphors" he claims, "mean what the words, in their most literal interpretation, mean and nothing more". The question of metaphor is pragmatic, not semantic: that is, it is the use of a literal statement in such a way as to "suggest" or "intimate", or "lead us to notice" What we might otherwise overlook. In a chapter on 'Metaphor" in Expression and Meaning (1979) John Searle proposed that to explain metaphor we must distinguish between "Word, or sentence meaning") (What the word or sentence means literally) and a speaker's "utterance meaning" (the metaphorical meaning that a speaker uses the literal word or sentence meaning to express). Searle goes on to propose a set of implicit principles, shared by the speaker and interpreter, to explain how a speaker can use a sentence with a literal meaning to say something with a very different metaphorical meaning as well as to clarify how a hearer recognizes and proceeds to interpret a literal sentence that is used metaphorically. When someone says, discussing Ran's eating habits, Ran is a pig", and when coleridge writes in the Ancient Mariner".

"The moonlight steeped in Silentness
The steady Weathercock".

We recognize that the noun 'Pig' and the verb 'steeped' are metaphors and have no problem understanding them.

But after twenty-five centuries of attention to metaphors by rhetoricians, grammarians and literary critics in which during the last half-century they have been joined by many philosophers-there is no general agreement about the way we identify metaphors, how we are able to understand them and what they serve to tell us.

Distinctive procedure in this view is to identify a number of "basic conceptual metaphors" that pervade discourse in our Western Culture, but are so common and operate so automatically that for the most part we use them without noticing them. Some of the most common basic metaphors are : Purposes Are Destinations; Time Moves; Time Is A Reaper; Life is a Journey; Life is A Play; People Are Plants. Such metaphors establish cross-conceptual mappings that manifest themselves in our ordinary speech as well as in the greatest poetry. People Are Plants, for example, is a type of cognitive mapping that underlies such everyday expressions as 'She's in the flower of youth," "She's a late bloomer," and "He's withering fast," no less than it does king lear's 'Ripeness is all".

Vigorous debates about metaphor continue apace. A plausible conclusion is that the diverse accounts of metaphor need not be mutually exclusive, in that each is directed especially to a particular one of many kinds of metaphor or functions of metaphor, or focuses on a different moment in the process of recognizing and understanding a metaphor, or is adapted to the particular perspective of a distinctive world view.

Symbolism

Symbolism may be defined as the use of any part or parts of a play, novel, or poetry like character, incident, setting, situation, language to suggest an idea or ideas not conveyed by the surface story. By the use of symbols the writer is able to enclose the vast concepts within little space. It enables him to suggest the deeper reality and the significance of his theme. It can 'also' be considered as an important aspect of, writer's technique of communication. Arthur Symons dedicated his book The Symbolist Movement in Literature to W.B. Yeats and called him 'the chief representative of that movement in our country'. Symbolism helps in giving concreteness to the visions. In Yeat's own words, "a symbol is (indeed) the possible expression of some invisible essence, a transparent lamp about a spiritual flame;..." Symbols are not merely denotative, but also connotative and evocative. In addition to the literal meaning, they also conjure up a host of associations before the mind's eye. According to Arthur Symons, "for symbolist poet Mallarme, to name is to destroy, to suggests to create Nathaniel Howtharne is also an influential great American Symbolist. He has used a symbol 'A' on the Hester Prynne's Bosom, which symbolically shows her as an adulterous. But she has changed her 'A', adulterous to 'A', able.

The passage in whitman's poem symbolises, first, the exploration through rail road and steamship. Secondly, it symbolises man's journey to the past of religion and fable. Thirdly, it symbolises his intellectual exploration to white the past, the present and the future. Fourthly, it symblises the spiritual exploration leading to a merger of the soul with the divine. The title of the poem is symbolic. 'Passage' stands not only for physical journey but spiritual also. Similarly 'India' Symbolises primal (original) thought which alone can solve all the mysteries both of the East and the West.

The same thing happens in O'Neill's works. Through the use of symbolism, O'Neill universalises its theme and extends the scope and meaning of his plays beyond the limits of realism. For example The Iceman Cometh by O'Neill is a play about the death of a salesman. The title of the play has a double and symbolic meaning—a surface meaning as well as a hidden religious significance.

In Yeats' poetry, there are two types of symbols the traditional and the personal. 'The Rose' is a traditional symbol of beauty and it has been used by poets from times immeroial. But 'The Rose' symbol types on a different meaning in Yeats' poems.

Symbolism makes it possible for the writers to express 'the richness of man's deeper reality which is something essentially mystical".

Euphemism

A Euphemism is a substitution of an agreeable or less offensive expression in place of one that may offend or suggest something unpleasant to the listener or in the case of doublespeak to make it less trouble some for the speaker. The deployment of euphemisms is a central aspect within the public application of political correctness. It may also be an alternative of a description of something or someone rather than the name, to avoid revealing secret, holy or sacred names to the uninitiated or to obscure the identity of the subject of a conversation from potential eavesdroppers. Some euphemisms are intended to amuse.

There is some disagreement over whether certain items are or are not euphemisms. For example, sometimes the phrase visually impaired is labeled as a politically correct euphemism for blind, however, visual impairment can be a broader term for those who have partial sight in one eye or for those with uncorrected poor vision, a group that would be excluded by the word blind. There are three antonyms of euphemism : dysphemism-cocophemism bend power word. Euphemisms for deities as well as for religious practices and artifacts date to the earliest of written records. Protection of sacred names, rituals and concepts from the uninitiated has always given rise to euphemisms, whether it be for exclusion of outsiders or the retention of power among selected practitioners. In other words, we can say that a euphemism is a 'nice' way of saying something whose right name has become too charged to use in polite company. Handicapped word is used for crippled, disadvantaged for the poor are examples of euphemisms.

Transformational Generative Grammar

Transformational Generative Grammar or Transformational Grammar is a Generative grammar especially of a natural language in Linguistics. It has been developed in a chomskyan tradition-this theory is associated with Noam Chomsky particular Chamsky's teacher Zellig Harris. Generative grammar attempts to define rules that can generate the infinite number of grammatical sentences possible in a language. It starts not from a behaviorist analyses of minimal sounds but from a rationalist assumption that a deep structure underlies a language and that a similar deep structure underlies all languages. Transformational grammar seeks to identify rules that govern relations between parts of a sentence on the assumption that beneath such aspects as word order a fundamental structure exists. Transformational and generative grammar together were the starting point for the tremendous growth in linguistics studies since 1950s. Theories of transformational generative grammar are intended as a model for the processes through which the human mind constructs and understand sentences. Chomsky made important proposal regarding how the success of grammatical theories should be evaluated. For example transformational grammar relates the active sentence. "John read the book' with its corresponding passive, "The book was read by John". The statement 'George

Saw Mary' is related to the corresponding questions, "Whom for who) did George see?" and "Who saw Mary?" Although sets such as these active and passive sentences appear to be very different on the surface, transformational grammar tries to show that in the 'underlying structure' (in their collations to one another), the sentences are very similar. This grammar assigns a 'deep structure' and a 'surface structure' to show the relationship of such sentences. Thus, 'I know a man who flies planes' can be considered the surface form of a deep structure approximately like 'I know a man. The man flies airplanes. ' The notion of deep structure can be easily helpful in explaining ambiguity of the sentence.

All ,languages have the same deep structure but they differ from each other in surface structure because of the application of different rules for transformations, pronunciation and word insertion.

ESP

English for specific purpose, term refers to teaching a specific genre of English for students with specific goals. ESP is English for vocational purposes, where the word Vocation is used loosely to include education and all kinds of employment. An ESP programme is therefore built on an assessment of purposes and needs and the functions for which English is required. It concentrates more on language in context than on teaching grammar and language structures. It covers subjects varying from accounting or computer Science to tourism and business management. The ESP focal point is that English is not taught as a subject separated from the students' real world; instead it is migrated into a subject matter area important to the learners. As a matter of fact, ESP combines subject matter and English language teaching. Such a combination is highly motivating because students are able to apply what they learn in their English classes to their main field of study. Being able to use the vocabulary and structures that they learn in a meaningful context reinforces what is taught and increases their motivation.

It the ESP class, students are shown how the subject matter context is expressed in English. The teacher can make the most of the students, knowledge of subject matter, thus helping them learn English faster, The term 'specific' in ESP refers to the specific purpose for learning English. Students approach the study of English through a field that is already known and relevant to them. This means that they are able to use what they learn in the ESP classroom right away in their work and studies. The ESP approach enhances the relevance of what the students are learning and enables them to use the English they know to learn even more English, since their interest in their field will motivate them to interact with speakers and texts. ESP assesses needs and integrates motivation, subject matter and content for the teaching of relevant skills.

Bilingualism

India has a long tradition of bilingualism. Bilingnalism refers to the proficiency in and use of more than one language. Till some time back it was believed that monolingualism or the use of one language was the norm in most parts of the world and that blingualism was some kind of unusual phenomenon. In recent times however it has been gradually realised that all of us are blinguals, because even where one is supposedly using only one language. One does control and employ several styles, registers and dialects of the same language. The term 'bilingualism' has now, however, come to be accepted as the standard cover term for referring to all situations involving two or more languages. A number of definitions of Bilingualism are available in the literature.

1. Bilingualism is "the practice of using two languages simultaneously" (Vriel Weinneich).

2. Bilingualism refers to "the simultaneous learning of two languages..." (Assenian).

One may begin leaning second language at a very young age almost as early as one learn first language or one may learn it at a later period in one's life in the literature on bilingualism we find a threefold distinction with regard to proficiency in second language. Researches by linguists, psycholinguists and others suggest that the subordinate bilingual is a person who has been taught the second language through the grammar translation method and is at the beginner's stage in his her control over the second language. He/she operates with a simple mechanism whereby items of mother-tongue (first language) are translated into equivalent items of second language. The next stage in bilingual proficiency is reached when one becomes a coordinate bilingual. The coordinate bilingual, it is suggested, operates with two separate semantic bases-one for first language and other for second language. This, rather than using the simple procedure of item-to-item translation, the coordinate bilingual seems to operate with two separate items and produces the matching linguist signs in the two languages concerned. The third kind of bilingual has been referred to as compound bilingual. This bilingual operates with a fused or single semantic base, a single set or represents and has complete control over the two linguistic codes, first language and second language. When two languages are learnt spoken and used by individuals and whole group or communities, they come to form a kind of co-existent system in the linguistic reportoire of the bilinguals. But where institutional and educational support is given to second language in a large measure it may come to be viewed as an imposition or an wanted burden. It may also happen that the second language is viewed as language of power, prestige and opportunity, leading to negative attitudes towards first language. In extreme cases such a situation may lead to partial or total loss of first language. Thus there are different aspects of blingualism that should be kept in mind. It is a complex and fascinating phenomenon.

Second Language acquisition

Second language Acquisition is the process by which people learn a second language in addition to their native languages. It is also called second language learning. Sometimes these terms are not treated as synonyms and are insted used to refer to the subconscious and conscious aspect of this process. Different models of SLA have focused on different aspects of SLA and general linguistic research. Schumann's Acculturation Model, which viewed second language acquisition as just one part of adapting to a new culture, emphasized findings related to language socialization. No single model of SLA has gained wide acceptance. Researchers have found a very consistent order in the acquisition of first language structures by children and this has drawn a great deal of interest from SLA scholars. Considerable efforts have been devoted to testing the identity hypothesis, which asserts that first language and second language acquisition conform to the same patterns. However orders of acquisition in SLA do often resemble those found in first language acquisition and may have common neurological causes. The study of the effects of teaching on second language acquisition seeks to systematically measure or evaluate the effectiveness of language teaching practices. Such studies have been undertaken for every level of language, from phonetics to pragmatics and for almost every current teaching methodology.

Handling Large Classes

large classes are often perceived as one of the major obstacles to ensuring quality education. We assume that learning occurs in proportion to class size. The smaller the class, the more students learn. Research shows that class size does not automatically correlate with student learning. Students in large classes can learn just as well as those in small ones. Handling large classes is a challenge. But it can also offer many opportunities for the teacher to improve his teaching. The value of a large class is that it contains a diversity of students and learning styles. There is no best way to teach large classes. A teacher must develop the approach that works best for him/her based on his teaching style, the characteristics, of his students and the goals and objectives of the lessons and curriculum. In large classes, teachers need an effective way to learn about their students' lives outside of the classroom so if learning problem arise, they can help the students as much as possible.

Giving each student the chance to talk in class during the first two or three weeks of school encourage them to participate in large class discussions. Students in large classes may not want to ask or answer questions because they fear showing others that they don't understand the concept. To help them overcome their fear, teacher should admit that it is difficult to understand the material for the first time. One of the biggest disadvantage of large classes is the high student-teacher ratio. One way to combat this problem is to be available to students before and after class.

The performance of students who require more guidance often suffer in large classes. This problem can be dealt with in many ways , such as tracking students' progress by reviewing their attendance, their performance on exams and homework, their participation in class and their performance of other classes. Teacher should choose rules that make the classroom environment orderly and promote successful learning. Students can be very helpful in managing a classroom's psycho-social environment. While planning the lesson, teacher can identify activities in which all of the students can participate. Students in large classes will be more attentive if they are exposed to a variety of learning activities and teaching strategies. Teaching a large class takes a great deal of time and energy. A wonderful lesson plan is needed. At the end of lecture, it is good to summarize important ideas. Good teachers should reflect on their teaching in large classes. Above all, teacher should view the challenge of teaching a large class as an opportunity not a problem.

Situational language Teaching

Situational language Teaching is an approach developed by British applied linguists in the 1930s to 1960s and which had an impact on language courses which service in some still being used today. It was discovered that languages have a core basic vocabulary of about 2000 words that occurred frequently in written text and it was assumed that mastery of these would greatly aid reading comprehension. Parallet to this was the notion of grammar control emphasizing the sentence patterns most commonly found in spoken conversation. The main purposed benefit was that such theoretically based organization of content would result in a less confusing sequence of learning events with better contextualization of the vocabulary and grammatical patterns presented. All language points were to be presented in situations. The theory of learning situation language Teaching is behaviorism, addressing moral the processes, than the conditions of learning. It includes the following principles :

1. Language learning is habit formation.
2. Mistakes are bad not should be avoided as they make bad habits.
3. Language skill are learned more effectively if they are presented orally first than in written form.
4. Analogy is a better foundation for language learning than analysis.
5. the Meanings of words can be learned only in a linguistic and cultural context.

Situational language teaching uses a structural syllabus and a word list. The procedure in of teaching it is typical. It move from oral use of sentence patterns to their automatic use in speech reading and writing. In Situational language Teaching, students learn to have a practical command of the four basic skills of a language, through structure. It helps to maintain accuracy in both pronounciation and grammar. It increases ability to respond quickly and accurately in speech situations. In short, Situational language Teaching was viewed as the basis of language and structure as being at the heart of speaking ability.

Literature and Gender (part-II)

1. Rebecca West
2. Mary wollstone craft's A Vindication of the Rights of the Women
3. Anita Desai's Fire on the Mountain
4. Kamala Das' My Story
5. Mahasweta Devi
6. A Feminist reading of Osbornels Look Back in Anger
7. Bharti Mukherjee
8. Gita Hariharan
9. George Eliot's Middlemarch
10. Kate Millett's Sexual Politics.

Rebecca West

Rebecca West, who is also known as cicely Isabel Fairfield, was born on 21 December 1892 and breathed her last on 15 March 1983. She got her recognization as an English author, journalist, literary critic and a travel writer. From the very childhood days she was inspired by books, music and lively company at her own home. She was greatly influenced by her mother, Isabella, a Scotswoman, a great pianist and her father charles fairfield, an Anglo Irish journalist. She became popular in her early days of career for an eloquent spokesman for feminist and socialist causes and for writing a number of essays and reviews for the New Republic, The Newyork Hearld Tribune, The New York American and The Daily Telegraph. George bernard Show said once about her that "Rebecca West could handle a pen as brilliantly as ever I could and much more savagely".

As she grew older, she gave a broader sense to the social and political issues. About feminism she says, "I myself have never been able to find out what feminism is, I only know that people call me a feminist whenever I express sentiments that different me from a doormat or a prostitute". Virginia woolf named Rebecca as the "arrent feminist" who offends men by saying they are snobs in *A Room of One's own.*

West worked on sequels to her autobiographically inspired novel The Fountain Overflows, but was not satisfied with the sequels and didn't publish them. Much of her work from the late phase of her life was posthumously, including Family Memories (1987), This Real Night (1984), Cousin

Rosamund (1985), The Only Poet (1992) and Survivors in Mexico (2003). She suffered from failing eyesight and high blood pressure in her last days. On hearing of her death, William Shown, the editor in chief of The New Yerker, said :

"Rebacca west was one of the giants and will have a lasting place in English literature. No one in this century wrote more dazzling prose, or had more wit or looked at the intricacies of human character and the ways of the world more intelligently".

Mary Wollstone Craft's A Vindication of the Rights of the Women

A Vindication of the Rights of Woman, written by the eighteenth century british feminist Mary Wollstonecraft, is one of the earliest works of feminist philosophy. This work is a response to those theories of the eighteenth century who didn't believe women should have an education. She believes that women are an important part of our Nation, because Men can only educate themselves, but women can educate their own children, their whole family, their whole Nation. By getting education they can also stand as a companion to their husbands, rather than mere wives. They are not mere ornaments to decorate. She was prompted to write the Rights of woman after reading Charles Maurice De Talleygrand -Perigord's 1791 report to the French National Assembly, which stated that women should only receive a domestic education. She dedicated her work to Talleyrand :

"Having read with great pleasure a pamphlet, which you have lately published, I dedicate this volume to you, to induce to reconsider the subject and naturally weight what I have advanced respecting the rights of woman and national education".

This work is an extension of Woolstonecraft's argument in the Rights of men, which is connected with rights of particular men of eighteenth century British men. But in rights of women she is not concerned with particular women but with rights of every woman. She argued that a woman must be intelligent in her own right. She maintained that this didn't contradict the role of woman as a mother or a career or the role of the woman in the home. She maintained that 'meek wives are, in general foolish mothers". She believed that if girls were encouraged from an early age to develop their minds, it would be seen that they were rational creatures and there was no reason whatsoever for them not to be given the same opportunities as boys with regard to education and training.

Women could enter the professions and have careers just the same as men.

In this book wollstonecraft attacked the educational restrictions that kept women in a state of ignorance and slavish dependence. She was especially critical of a society that encouraged women to be "docile and attentive to their looks to the exclusion of all else". She described marriage as "legal prostitution". The ideas in this book are truly revolutionary and caused tremendous controversy stating in her preface that my main argument is built on this simple principle, that if (woman) be not prepared by education to become the companion of man, she will stop the progress of knowledge and virtue, for truth must be common to all, Wollstonecraft contends that society will degenerate without educated women, particularly because mothers are the primary educators of young children.

Fire On the Mountain

Anita Desai has undoubtedly been recognized as one of the prominent voices among Indian writers in English. Her consistent involvement of more than three and a half decades in the field of fiction has won her wide critical acclaim in India and abroad. The recipient of Sahitya Academy Award for her novel Fire on the Mountain in 1978, Desai had also been awarded the coveted Padama Shri in January 1989. She has written about a dozen novels and two short story books.

Desai has often been claimed as novelist of the inner landscape. Her main foothold is the exploration of the deep recesses of human psyche, going beyond the skin into the constant struggles raging the soul of human beings at the conscious and the sub-conscious level and describing the atmosphere of the mind. She emphasis on interior than on exterior characterization; on motives and circumstances and on the invisible than visible. All her characters are constantly struggling either against individuals, against social environment or even against own inner selves. She also focuses upon the female trauma in her novels. She has also followed the tradition of stream of consciousness in her fiction to show the conflict between the inner and the outer self.

The novel fire on Mountain (1977) reveals that the book can well be interpreted as the three different facet of the inner consciousness as reflected through Nanda Kaul, ILA Das and Raka. The seclusion and alienation from society leave different impressions on all the three souls, who are highly sensitive and emotional. There is a vast difference between their names, desires, dreams and hard outside facts of life.

Nanda Kaul could never feel a sense of belongingness in Husband's house which was always Mr. Kaul's house. Her life was of un-fulfillment, deprivations and frustrations. It was a life of abundance in everything but love and faith, which she detested most. The shortage of privacy always vexed her. And her longing for a peaceful life forced her to withdraw from the outside world. In her solitary life, she pretends to live happily. But this is not the real truth of her existence. After Mr. kaul's death she settled down in the secluded surrounding of corignano, in kasauli kills to keep her privacy alive. There she comes to know about her grand daughter Raka's arrival. She suddenly bursts out :

"Discharge me... I have discharged
All my duties. Discharge".

At Raba's arrival she realizes that she is growing more and more fond of Raka. The need to reclaim Raka's love is an expression of Nanda's unconscious desire to love and be loved. The barren mountain put to fire by little Raka is no one else but Nanda herself.

Thus the total withdrawl and negation of life can never provide any heaving touch to the wounded souls and shattered selves. It means the withdrawal of Nanda Kaul from active outside life was not self-imposed. In short in Desai's novel we are confronted with the searching sensibility of her sensitive characters and witness their attempt to find a choerent rationale of existence.

Kamala Das' My Story

Kamala Das is the most outstanding, distinctive and original Indian poet writing in English today. All her poetry belongs to self. As Paul Vergheese points out, "Her strength as well as her weekness as a poet consists in the fact that she is most herself and cannot be referred to literary influences. If this gives her an individuality and a personal meaning, it also leads her to lapse of tact and a general looseness in verse structure. Otherwise in her poetry we have an expression of female sensibility at its best". She has always kept her very self in the centre of her works. She talks about her love-longings, frustrations, desires and unfulfillment of those desires very frankly without any hesitation. Her Autobiography My Story tells us very much about her poetry and her themes to mountain the individuality and feminine identity.

Kamala Das was born at Punnayarkulam in Malabar in Kerala in 1934. She got the poetry as an inheriditary because her parents were poets. In most of her poems, she talked about her grandmother because of very much attachment to her. She couldn't get the regular education from school or college but got it at very home. She got married at an early age of her life but was not satisfied and happy with her married life because of the age difference. Although she got the fatherly attention from her husband. And we see all this dissatisfaction and unhappiness in her autobiographical novel, My Story.

My Story, an autobiographical novel by Kamala Das,

was published in 1976. It contains the clear picture of her life, her frank discussion about the quest of love inside and outside the marriage. She talks about extra marital affair very frankly which makes her autobiography very controversial. But it is a perfect example of her far sightedness, because whatever she has revealed at that time, is still prevalent in this period. In its preface she claims that the book had caused her some pain but she wished "to empty herself of all her secrets, so that I could depart when the time came with a scrubbed out conscience".

Kamala Das is bilingual and writes easily in Malayalam and English. She is also known as a feminist writer. As an artist her paintings include nudes. In 1999, she converted to Islam, because she believed that only Islam gives protection to women. Islam is the only religion in the country that gives love and protection to women.

Thus in her works, Kamala Das the woman and Kamala Das the artist become one, and the personal experience is universalized. And Love with many facets has remained as a centre of her poetry.

Mahasweta Devi

Mahasweta Devi sincerely believes that, "a responsible writer, standing at a turning point in history, has to take a stand in defense of the exploited. Her writings provide scope for viewing her work from the feminist angle. Mahasweta Devi, the Bengali activist writer and the recipient of Jananpith award for the year 1999 stands unique among Indian writers in portraying the societal and governmental/ State Violations of human rights to Dalits, tribals, women and children. Her plays give a reflection of social realism because it has given her dramatic art verisimilitude, has also infused her work with breath of life and has allowed the maximum opportunity to comment. Through her writings she has tried her best to focus the attention of urban people on the hidden realistic from which they are totally unaware.

Her non-dramatic writings especially activist writings also reveal her concern for human rights. The collection of her writings (42 novels, 15 collections of stories, a collection of plays and hundred of articles) document the struggles of the subalterns, especially untouchables, for their basic human rights.

Mahaswets Devi's plays are after located in the communities of the fringe outside the uppercaste milieu. The fringe dewellers, particularly the untouchables form the focus of her story. From 1976 onwards, Mahaswets has become more and more involved with the lives and struggles of the tribal and underprivileged communities settled in the border regions of the three neighboring states of West Bengal. She says, "I have found authentic documentation to be the best medium for protest against injustice and exploitation.

In her play Urvashi O Johnny, by adding, passages of poetic beauty and a number of popular songs, Mahasweta Devi has achieved the depth and intensity which otherwise would have been impossible. She has tried to create a realistic atmosphere on the stage by being faithful to the life styles of the characters she deals with. About her another play Aajir she herself says : 'I got the idea of Aajir from a slave bond executed by a slave who sold himself into slavery. Her play Mother of 1084, is a moving story of a mother, apathetic, apolitical and pathetically ignorant of her own son and his ideals. Through the character of mother, Mahasweta Devi seeks to bring to light the darker areas of life where persecution of the innocent continues unabated.

Even at the age of 73, she continues to be a writer thus by lending voice to the voiceless, Mahasweta Devi emerges as a fighter for human rights.

Feminist Reading in Look Back in Anger

Look Back in Anger (1956) was first staged at the Royal Court Theatre in 1956 and it was at once hailed as "an angry play by an angry young man," and John Osborne was called the creator of "the angry young man movement". This play is a study of the quest for solidarity in married life on the part of a young intellectual from the working classes. This makes the play a penetrating study of a perverse and unhealthy marriage relationship. Osborne has successfully captured the mood of despair and frustration of the postwar generation.

The actual action of the play is centered around Jimmy Porter's relationship with his wife Alison and his anarchism here develops into the familiar pattern of love/hate relationship between the sexes. Deeply in love, the young couple is perpetually inflicting wounds on each other, until eventually the wife feels she can bear no more. She finally leaves him. Her place is taken by her friend Helena Charles who also feels the same ambivalence in her love for Jimmy moving in her case from hatred to love. Osborne brings out very well the appalling side of all this self-destruction which continues until the calm of desolation is established and the tragedy of Jimmy Porter is paralleled by that of his wife. Alison gives the reader the impression of a young lady going through life with an expression of complete bafflement and bewilderment etched on her face. Her marriage with Jimmy brings about an astounding change in her social world. It is only after marriage that she becomes aware of Jimmy's deep rooted class prejudice, his hatred and detestation of the upper class of which she is a member. She then realizes that Jimmy's marrying her was more akin to revenge than to love. Through his marriage, he had sought to avenge himself upon the upper classes by reducing away from them a member of their class. What little of love encouraged his marriage appeared to evaporate soon after Jimmy and his friend High Tanner came to regard her as a hostage from the upper classes. Alison finds it difficult to accept this role but there is nothing she can do about it. Alison does not have the intellectual fortitude to stand up to Jimmy's unremitting, perpetual insults flung at her family and her social world. Whatever the subject being discussed Jimmy finds ways and mean of turning into an insult to her father or her mother. She cannot repel these violent thrusts. Silence is her only alternative. She never really learns to adopt his set of values and abandon the ones inculcated in her since birth`

If Alison's emotional catharsis is evident to a lesser extent Helena undergoes a similar evolution. Helena schemed to usurp Alison's role. Her lack of solidarity to a fellow woman, Allison is about as anti-feminist as one can get. Yet, she does atone for this in her understanding that what she did was wrong and that she should leave. This solidarity shown to Alison, a fellow woman represents the Feminist desire to create community and strength with one another as opposed to being divided by the larger social order. In the end, Alison realizes that Jimmy had wanted her to feel pain, suffering and deprivation so that she may wake up out of her intellectuous lethargy and see the world as it is. Finally, Jimmy accepts her.

Bharti Mukherjee

Bharti Mukherjee's approach to life and its problems is deeply rooted in her Indian background. She was born in 1940 into a Bengali family and had received a traditional education. Born into a Hindu Bengali Brahmin family she had different sense of self of existence, and of morality than other writers. Her belief that soulds can be reborn, makes her different from other American writers, who believe to have only one life. Her different but traditional view is evident in her portrayal of women characters in her novels. Inspite of having Indianness in mind and spirit, she has sketched several pictures of arrogant men and docile women, who some times desires to transcend the conventional norms but gets failed. She shows in her novels the constricting influence of gender stereotypes on the invidualilty of girls as well as on their social behaviour.

Bharti Mukherjee is not only a novelist but also a essayist, short story writer and nonfiction writer. At present she is a professor in the department of English at the University of California, Berkeley. She has nationality of India, United States and Canada from where she received the degree of B.A., M.A. and M.F.A. She received her Ph.D. degree from the University of Lowa, where she met the Canadian writer Clerk Blaise whom she married in 1963. She has been described as a writer who has lived through different phases of life. Firstly she lives as a Colonial, then led a life of exile as a post Colonial in Canada and finally shifted as an immigrant and then as a citizen of United States. Her main concern in her novels is to show the condition of Asian immigrants in North America with a particular focus to the changes takes place in South Asian Women in a new world. In her novel Jasmine, she also shows an Indian refugee who is empowered by the trials of assimulation and the Indian refugee is a girl who is widowed at an early age of her life and shifted to America. She was awarded by National Book critics circle Award for her best work *The Middleman and Other Stories,* (1988) which was a collection of short stories.

The Tiger's Daughters (1971) is Mukherjee's very first novel in which she explores the feelings of culture shock of a female protagonist, Tara, who was raised in calcutta, educated in New York and is married to an American man, after her travelling back to India. In her novel *wife,* she again shows the story of a couple, who have moved to United States and experience culture shock and loneliness. In her one of the best novels *Desirable Daughters.* She sets herself a dual task : She wants to tell her Indian readers about those Indians who are in America and her American readers about the customs and traditions that are followed by the Indian Society.

Her literary agenda, Mukherjee has written, "begins by acknowledging that America has transformed me. It does not end until I show how I (and the hundreds and thousands like me) have transformed America." Thus she has developed an international recognization for exploring through her works, the meeting of the third world and the first from the perspective of the immigrant to North America to Canada and to the United States.

She has tried her best in reflecting her personal experiences in crossing cultural boundaries in her writings.

Geeta Hariharan

The winner of commonwealth writers prize for the best First Book, *The Thousands Faces of the Night,* Geeta Hariharan was born in 1954 and educated in Mumbai, Manila and the United States. She is one of the prominent writers among Indian English writers. She got her three novels published in a wick succession, for which she worked over a period of ten years. About the inspiration, she said in an interview that each work begins differently. Sometimes it is an idea that tantalize me so much that I have to flesh it out. Sometimes it is a character or an image or a situation once I have a beginning that holds me, I do a lot of groundwork-planning, reading and making detailed notes. Then I take the plunge. About Geeta hariharan, Michael Ondatje, says, "Gita Hariharn's fiction is wonderful, full of subtleties and humor and tenderness. J.M. Coetzee described her as, "An outstanding writer".

She got the worldwide recognization through her works like The Árt of Dying, The Ghost of Vasu Master when Dreams Travel, The Winning Team, A Southern harvest and Fugitive Histories. *The Thousand Faces of Night,* was a story of the old servant woman and in *The Ghosts of Vasu Master,* she tells the story of the old man and a little boy. She describes how the old man certainly learns a lot about himself in teaching the silent little boy. (She also got this novel nominated for commonwealth writers prize in 1995. In her latest novel *Fugitive Histories,* She exposes the legacy of prejudice in India today. She has herself said that all my novels and stories look at power politics in some way or the other. Fiction has thousand ways of giving us a new take on the dynamics of power relations. The Business Standard writes about her, "There is nothing loose about Hariharn's writing. Her sentences are controlled, all extra words shaved away. The distilled brevity is delightful, the unsaid hovers everywhere. She worked as a staff writer in WNET-Channel 13 in New York and also worked as an editor in Bombay, Madras and New Delhi.

George Eliot's Middlemarch

Middlemarch : A study of Provincial life (1874) is a novel written by George Eliot (1819-1880). She was an English novelist of the Victorian era. Her real name was Nary Anne Evans. She used a male pen name for better consideration of her works. Her novels are famous for their realism and psychological insight. The novel Middlemarch is notable for its deep psychological insight and sophisticated character portraits. As the title suggests the novel is set in the fictitious midlands town of Middlemanch during the period 1830-32. The Central Character in the novel is a beautiful young woman Dorothea Brooke who marries an older man Causbon and finds he is not at all that he imagined. The couple lives unhappily. She without the intellectual stimulation desperately craves. The serious conflict in their relationships begins as soon as causbon's nephew will Ladislaw enters their lives. Dorothea feels attracted towards him. Contrasted with this is the tale of Doctor Lydgate and his marriage to a bright young socialite who ruins him-Rosamond. Rosamond is complete opposite of Dorothea and Dr. Lydgate the opposite of causbon, where are many other lives, loves and intriguers. In the end Dorothy is warded with true love and Du. Lydgate is rewarded with the saving of his career. It has many plots and strong romantic elements.

This novel has many themes like the status of women in society, nature of marriage, political reform and education. It has many characters. This book examines how education affects the characters. Class climbing is also a theme of the novel as there are distinct social classes based on birth and money. Most of the characters live in imagination and try to live in their imagination. As Dorothea wants nothing in life but good. She rejects a young man who would have been a reasonably good match for her. She marries the aged scholar Mr. Casaubon Eliot expresses an extremely pessimistic view of humanity with the theme of debt and money throughout Middlemarch. The writer concludes that Middlemarch represents the spirit of nineteenth century England through its characters.

Kate Millett's Sexual Politics

The world wide recognized book *Sexual Politics* by Kate Millet made her famous all over the world as an American feminist writer and activist. It is considered as her best book. It is actually originated as her Ph.D. dissertation awarded by Columbia University in 1970. In this Millett Critiques the Sexism and heterosexism of the modern novelists contrasting with the view points of the homosexual authors. She also visited Iran to work for women's rights and wrote about her experiences in her book *Going to Iran.*

In Introducing the term "Sexual Politics", one must answer the inevitable question, "Can the relationship between the sexes be viewed in a political light at all. The answer depends on how one takes or defies politics. In this book Politics does not refer to a narrow and exclusive world of meetings, chairmen and parties. Here Politics means power structured relationships, arrangements one group of persons is controlled by another.

It is time we gave attention to defining a theory of politics which treats of power relationships on the less formal than establishmentarian grounds of personal intercourse between members of well defined and coherent groups-races, castes, classes and sexes. It is precisely because such groups have no representation in formal political structures that their oppression is so entire and so continuous. Why, when this arrangement of male rule and control of our society is so obvious, why is it never discussed. Why does no one remark that every thing related to power in our culture including the repressive forces of the police-entirely in male hands. Money, guns, authority, everything is limited to Male. Even God is male. Let us wake up and have a purpose. All of us Black, white and gold, male, female, have it, within our power to create a world we could bear out of the desert we inhabit for we held our fate in our own hands. This book not only explored history but also became a part of it.

Millet says sexual domination is the most pervasive ideology of our culture and provides its most fundamental concepts of power. She asserts "The essence of politics is power". The ruling sex maintains and extends its power over subordinate sex. This process is pervasive throughout cultural life. Her work is certainly a significant milestone in feminist literature. She expected feminism to be fully conscious, morally and politically correct-it must know what it wanted.

Course XX Option (II)
Literature and Philosophy

1. George Bernard shaw's Man and Superman
2. Bergson's creative Evolution
3. Sri Aurobindo
4. Jalal ad-Din Mahammad Rumi
5. Pablo Neruda
6. Iris Murdoch's The Sea, the Sea
7. Milan Kundera's Ignorance
8. Franz Kafka The Metamorphosis
9. Michel Focault
10. Jacques Derrida

George Bernard show's Man and Superman

Man and Superman (1903) is a famous play penned by George Bernard Shaw. Although Man and Superman can be performed as a light comedy of manners but show intended the drama to be something much deeper as suggested by the title. The title comes from Friedrich Nietzsche's philosophical ideas about the Ubermensch (Superman). This famous romantic comedy tells the story of two rivals : John Tanner (a wealthy, politically-minded intellectual who values his freedom) and Ann Whitefield (a charming, scheming hypocritical young woman who wants tanner as a husband). Once Tanner realizes that Miss Whitefield is hunting for a spouse and that he is the only target), he attempts to flee from her, only to find out that his attraction to Ann is too overwhelming to escape. Octavius loves Ann and wants to marry her but Ann rejects Octavius's marriage proposal time and again. Octavius indicates that he will spend the rest of his life mourning this rejection. Ann then wool and win Jack Tanner, despite his recognizing he wiles with which she ensnares him. They find compatibility in cynicism. Printed play includes a dedication in the form of a letter addressed to Arthur Bingham Walky, a drama critic and Shaw's friend of fifteen years, who according to the letter, had once asked shaw why he did not write a Don Juan play. The dedication defends the play's 'preaching' tone and sets out the premise of the play as 'the natural attraction of the sexes," to be distinguished from a play about love or marriage. The rest of the rather long and digressive letter explains that Don Juan is a philosopher who follows his instincts, along with some of his theories. This is a play admittedly designed for 'a pit of philosopher' as audience.

This play contains an explicit articulation of a major Shavian theme. Man is the spiritual creator, whereas woman is the biological 'life force' that must always triumph over him. Ann whitefield is referred to as the 'Life Force' and represents shaw's view that in every culture, it is the women who force the men to marry them rather than the men who take the initiative.

Bergson's Creative Evolution

Creative evolution (1907) is written by a French philosopher Henry Louis Bergson. Its English translation appeared in 1911. It is undoubtedly the most widely known and most discussed of his books. It constitutes one of the most profound and original contributions to the philosophical consideration of evolution. Bergson's popularity increased enormously not only in academic circles but among the general reading public. He was awarded Nobel Prize in Literature in 1927. *The Creative Evolution* provides an alternate explanation for Darwin's mechanism of evolution, suggesting that evolution is motivated by a vital impetus that can also be understood as humanities natural creative impulse. The book was very popular in the early decades of the twentieth century. The book develops concepts of time which significantly influenced modernist writers and thinkers. Bergson suggests that the experience of time as 'duration' can best be understood through Creative intution, not through intellect. In Creative Evolution, Bergson turned to biological considerations, he held that change means growth, growth means creation means freedom and if freedom was ultimately real what a liberation that spelled for the soul of man, no longer bound by the fixites of space, of logic and of habit! Bergson's theory of time and memory becomes a critique of purposes and ends in the logic and metaphysics of both idealism and mechanism and of both mechanical and vitalistic evolution. Evolution moves to no fixed ends and on the other hand it is more than advance by mechanical Darwinian elimination. Evolution is the expression of a creative urgency, a fulfillment of novel ends inventively generated in the process of time itself. Bergson's critique of the purely intellectual analysis of the idealists and the purely geometrical analysis of the materialists is shrewd criticism.

Bergson reinvigorated the theory of evolution by refusing to see it as merely mechanistic. His expansion on Derwin remains one of the most original and important philosophical arguments for a scientific inquiry still under fire today. He uses detailed scientific arguments as well as philosophical ones, but it is unclear that he can say why evolution takes the path that is does (or any coherent path) and is not merely chaotic.

Sri Aurobindo (1872-1950)

Sri Aurobindo was born in Kolkata. He was a poet, philosopher, nationalist and freedom fighter. He also joined the movement for India's freedom from British rule and became one of the most important leaders. He turned to develop his own vision and philosophy of human progress and spiritual evolution. He also passed the ICS Examination. Aurobindo joined state service working first in the survey and settlements department, later moving to the department of revenue and then to the Secretariat. He engaged in a deep study of Indian Culture, teaching himself Sanskrit, Hindi and Bengali. He published his first collections of poetry. 'The Rishi' from Baroda. He started taking interest in politics. His conversion from political action to spirituality occurred gradually. Aurobindo had been influenced by Bankim's Anandmath. Disturbances to his progress following the recent events surrounding the congress had put him in the need of consulting a Yogi. Aurobindo's observable political career lasted only four years, from 1906 to 1910. Though he had been active behind the scene surveying. Organizing and supporting the nationalist cause ever since his return to India.

One of Sri Aurobindo's main philosophical achievements was to introduce the concept of evolution into Vedantic thought. He rejected a major conception of Indian philosophy that says that the World is a Maya (illusion) and that living as a renunciate was the only way out. He says that it is possible, not only to transcend human nature but also to transform it and to live in the world as a free and evolved human being with a new consciousness and a new nature which could spontaneously perceive truth of things and proceed in all matters on the basis of inner oneness, love and light. A central tenet of Sri Aurobindo's philosophy is that the Truth of existence is an omnipresent Reality that both transcends the manifested universe and is inherent in it. He argues that Man is born an ignorant, divided, conflicted being; as a result, he does not know the nature of Reality including its source and purpose. What his individual and spiritual potential is amongst others. He laid utmost stress on finding and living in the Psychic being within which is the essence of our individual being.

In poetry, his principal work is 'Savitri-a legend and a symbol. The principal writings of Sri Aurobindo include in prose The life Divine, considered his single great work of metaphysics. The synthesis of Yoga, Secrets of the Vedas, Essays on the Gita, The Human Cycle, The Ideal of Human Unity, Renaissance in India and Other Essays, Supramental manifestation upon Earth, The Future Poetry, Thoughts and Aphorisms and several volumes of letters.

Jalalad Din Muhammad Rumi (1207-1273)

Jalal-ad-Din Muhammad Balkhi is also known as Jalal ad Din Muhammad Rumi. In English speaking world he is simply known as Rumi. He was a 13th century Persian poet, jurist, theologian and sufi myztic. Rumi is a descriptive name meaning 'the Roman' since he lived most of his life in an area called Rum. He was born in Balkh in present day Afghanistan. Rumi practiced suffism as a disciple of Burhan ud-Din until the later died. Rumi's public life then began, he became a teacher who preached in the mosques of Konya and taught his adherents in the madrassa. In December 1273, Rumi fell ill, he predicted his own death and composed the well-known ghazal which begins with the verse.

'How does't thou know what sort of king I have within me as a companion?

Do not cast thy glance upon my golden face, for I have iron legs".

He died on December 17, 1273 in Konya. A splendid shrine the Yesil Turbe/Green Tomb today the Mevlana Museum) was created over his place of burial. His epitaph reads :

When we are dead, seek not our tomb in the earth, find it in the hearts of men.

The general theme of Rumi's thought, like that of other mystic and Sufi poets of Persian literature is essentially that of the concept of 'tawhid'—union with his beloved from which/whom he has been cut off and become aloof and his longing and desire to restore it. He believed passionately in the use of music, poetry and dance as a path for reaching God. For Rumi, music helped devotees to focus their whole being on the divine and to do this so intensely that the soul was both destroyed and resurrected. He played a huge role in converting Orthodox Anatolia to Islam. His influence can be found in many if Islamic Clerics and their poetic work. Rumi's works has been translated into many of the world's languages, including Russian, German, Urdu, Turkish, Arabic, French, Italian and Spanish, and is being presented in a growing number of formats.

Rumi's poetry is often divided into various categories : the Quartrains and Odes of the Divan, the six books of the Masnavi. The prose works are divided into the Discourses, The Letters and the Seven Sermons. Rumi's major work is Ma Dnawiye Ma'nawi (Spiritual Couplets) regarded as the Persian-language Quran. It contains 27000 lines of persian poetry, other major work is the Diwan-e-Kabir on Diwan-e-Shams-Tabriz (The works of Shams of Tabriz). Besides approximately 35000 persian couplets and 2000 persian quartrains, the Divan contains 90 Ghazals and 19 quartrains in Arabic and many poems of mixed Persian and Turkish). His prose works are Fihi Ma Fihi (In It What's in It.), Majales-e-Sab'a (Seven Sessions, Makatib (The letters.) The Letters testify that Rumi kept very busy helping family members and administering a community of disciples that had grown up ground them.

Pablo Neruda

Pablo Neruda (1904-1973) was born in the town of Parral in Chilie. His real name is Jeftali Ricardo Reyes Bosoalto. In 1920, he became a contributor to the literary journal [Selva Austral' under the pen name of Pablo Neruda which he adopted in memory of the Czechoslovak poet Jan Neruda (1834-1891). Hse assumed his pen name as a teenager partly to hide his poetry from his father. Between 1927 and 1935, the government put him in charge of a number of honorary consulships, which took him to Burma, Ceylon, Java, Singapore, Bnenos Aires etc. His poetic production during that difficult period included, among other works, the collection of esoteric surrealistic poems. Residencia en la tierra (1933) which marked his literary breakthrough. His first book crepuscalario Twilight (1923) was privately printed. In 1924 Neruda published his book Veinte Poems de amoryuna Cancion desesperada (Twenty Love poems and a song of Despair, (1869) became a best seller. With this book Neruda became one of Latin America's most famous young poets.

In 1939, Neruda he wrote his *Canto General de Chile.* It compaises 250 poems. He transformed this book into an epic poem about the whole South American area, its nature its people and its historical destiny into general was translated into some ten languages. The central theme of the book is the struggle for social justice. In this work, Neruda examines Latin American history and shows his deep knowledge about the history, geography and politics of Latin America. His some other famous works are; Las Uyas Yel Vieinto (1954). Odas Elementales (1954-1959). Cien Sonetos de amor (1959) Arte de Pajaros (1966) La Barcarola (1967) Fin del Mundo (1969). Las Piedral del cielo 1970), para Nacer he Nacido (1977), Late and Posthumous Poems 196801975 (1988) etc.

Neruda's poetry exerted an enormous influence throughout Latin America and he remains beloved in his native chile. Many of his peoms about Spain are moving, whether they are elegies or fierce attacks, but many are propaganda pieces that have lost any power they may have had Time has revealed a dark side to Neruda's work. Some of his overtly political poems express a blood thirsty desire for venglance. Women are symbolic vehicles for the poet's salvation and self-discovery. Neruda considered himself primarily a love poet.

Iris Murdoch The Sea, The Sea

The Sea, the Sea' (1978) is a famous novel of Iris Murdoch whose full name is Dame Iris Murdoch (1919-1999). She was an Irish author and philosopher. She is a well-known novelist who wrote about sexual relationship, morality and the power of the unconscious.

The sea, the sea' novel won booker prize in the same year of its publication. Charles Arrow by is the central character of the novel. He decides to leave the world and starts living in seclusion in a house by the sea. Suddenly, he encounters Mary Hartley Fitch, his first love. He has not seen her since his love affair with Mary. When he meets Mary Hartley. She is unrecognisable as she has grown old Charles. Once again becomes obsessed by her and outside his theatrical world, idealizes his former relationship with her. He persuades her to elope with him. Charles is unable to recognise the selfishness and egotism of his own romantic ideals. Contrasting the thoughts and motivations of Hartley and her all too banally brutal husband been with those of Charles and his many neurotic visitors, the novel ascends into a whirlpool of opposing wills and stratgems.

The sea, the sea lays out a world of supernatural power, magic and illusion. Charles turns his back to the dazzling world of theatre and retreates to house by the sea to take stock of himself writes his memoir and makes a lasting treatment. He believes that he is eschewing the vulgar, self absorbed power plays that constituted his adult life as a director. He believes that he is learning to be good. But self-regard and manipulation of others are not so easy to get rid of. His egotism follows him. Murdoch elaborates one of a motives in her life long concern that with good with love and with Freedom to be good, one must transform the personal into the impersonal, one must escape one's private self and concern oneself with others. In the end the novel explains the risk and self-deceptions of the spiritual life, the important distinction between imagination and fantasy and the vital importance of negotiating these dangers.

Ignorance by Milan Kundera

Ignorance, a novel written by Milan Kundera, first published in 2000 in French, was translated into English in 2002. The novel is set in 1989 after the communists have fallen in prague. The main protagonists are Irena and Josef, both emigrants, returning to Czechoslovkia for the first time in decades. The novel examines the feelings realized by the return to a homeland, which has ceased to be a home. Kundera has presented a picture of love and its manifestations. He explores that people have selective memories as a precursor to ignorance. He offers an insight into exile and memory. Kundera has also tried to show his own experiences in his novel, as he himself moved to France. He emigrated when he was forty six years old, because his situation in Czechoslovabia was very difficult. So this theme of emigration and exile was always very important for him. He focuses on two characters Joseph, coming from Denmark and Ireana, who is coming from Paris with her Swedesh boyfriend on return she feels that none of her old Czech friends are interested in her French experience. She realized that they are showing no interest in what she was trying to tell them. She soon sees that their questions are of a particular kind. They ask questions to check whether are knows what they know, whether she remembers, what they remember. This has a effect on her, one that will stay with her. She feels more lost than before when she discovers that people really aren't interested in her experience of exile. In the end two characters meet. Irena remembers him very affectionately. She can remember meeting him one night, but he cann't remember her at all. For Joseph, Irena just symbolizes some moments of pleasure without a future. Kundera has presented very beautifully the themes of emigation, nostalgia, and changes in memory. The book offers a philosophical discourse on the nature of emigration and the feelings a great return can provoke.

Franz Kafka's The Metamorphosis

The Metamorphosis (1915) is a beautiful novella written by Franz Kafka. Franz Kafka (1883-1924) was a German fiction written of the early 20th century. During his life time he published only a few short stories and never finished his novels. The metamorphosis is exception as it is considered a short novel. The Central figure of this novella is Gregor Samsa. He is a travelling salesman. One day when he wakes up he finds himself transformed into a giant insect. Now he worries about his job as he is the only financial source for his parents and sister, Grete. His appearance horrifies his family. His sister provides him water and stale rotton food. As George remains a devoted and loving son, he hides himself beneath a sofa whenever someone enters his room. Now his parents do not rely upon his income, they take on jobs and Grate's caretaking deteriorates. One day, his father pelts him with apples. One of the apples becomes embedded in his back and causes an infection.

His parents use Gregor's room as a dumping area for unwanted objects. Gregor becomes dirty. One day he slowly walks into the dinning room the lodgers see him and refuse to pay the rent. Gregor's family determine that the insect is no longer Gregor and plan to get rid of it. Gregor returns to his room and due to his wound, dies. As the family members see the corpse, they feel a burden has been lifted from them. They start planning for the future again. They don't feel any financial weakness at all. They forget Gregor easily.

The opening sentence of the novella is famous in English.

"When Gregor Samsa woke up one morning from unsettling dreams, he found himself changed in his bed into a monstrous vermin".

Kafka made extensive use of a trait special to the German language. He wrote so long sentences that sometimes took an entire page. Translations face difficulties in dealing with the author's intentional use of ambiguous terms of words that have several meanings.

Michel Foucault

Michel Foucault (1926-1984) was a French philosopher, sociologist and historian. He is best known for his critical studies of social institutions as well as for his work on the history of human sexuality. His personal life was difficult. He suffered from acute depression. As a result, he was taken to see a psychiatrist. During this time, Foucault became fascinated with psychology. He earned a licence (degree equivalent to B.A.) in psychology, a very new qualification in France at the time in addition to a degree in philosophy in 1952. In 1960s Foucault was associated with Structuralism, a movement from which he distanced himself. He rejected the post-structuralist and post modernist labels to which he was often later attributed. He is particularly influenced by the work of Nietzsche; his genealogy of knowledge is a direct allusion to Nietzsche's Genealogy of morals. In 2007 Foucault was listed as the most cited intellectual in the humanities by 'The Times Higher Education Guide. In his later years, he refused to identify himself as a philosopher, historian, structuralist or Marxist maintaining that 'The main interest in like and links to become someone else that you were not in the beginning". He rather desired his books "to be a kind of tool-box which others can rummage through to find a tool which they can use however they wish in their own area... I don't write for an audience, I write for users not readers". Foucault died of an Aids related illness in Paris. His famous works are :

1. Madness and Civilization : the first major book, examines ideas, practices, institutions art and literature relating to madness in Western history. Foucault argues that madness was silenced by reason, losing its power to signify the limits of social order and to point to the truth.

2. The Birth of the Clinic : An Archaeology of medical Perception (1963) translated into English in 1973. This book traces the development of the medical profession. Its motif is the concept of the medical regard, traditionally limited to small, specialized institutions such as hospitals and prisons.

3. Death and the Labyrinth: The world of Raymond Roussel was published in 1963 and translated into English in 1986. It is unique being Foucault's only work in literature. Foucault explores theory, criticism and psychology through the texts of Raymond Roussel, one of the fathers of experimental writing.

4. The order of things : An Archaeology of the Human Sciences (1970). The work broadly aims to provide an anti humanist excavation of the human sciences, such as sociology and psychology.

The Archaeology of knowledge (1969), Discipline and Punish (1977), The History of Sexuality (1984) are other important works of Michel Foucault.

Jacques Derrida

Jacques Derrida (1930-2004) is known as father of deconstruction. He was a French philosopher. His best known work is 'Of Grammatology' He first received major attention outside France with his lecture, 'Structure, Sign and Play in the Discourse of the human Sciences', delivered at John Hopkins University in 1966. The conference at which this paper was delivered was concerned with structuralism, then at the peak of its influence in France, but only beginning to gain attention in the United States. He praised the accomplishments of structuralism but also maintained reservations about its internal limitations, thus leading to the notion that his thought was a form of post-structuralism. The effect of Derrida's paper was such that by the time the conference proceedings were published in 1970, the title of the collection had become The Structuralist Controversy. Derrida's interests traversed disciplinary boundaries, and his knowledge of a wide array of diverse material was reflected in the tree collections of work published in 1967. Speech and phenomena, of Grammatology and Writing and Difference. These three books contained readings of the work of many philosophers and authors including Husserl, linguist De Saussure, Heidegger, Rousseau, Hegal, Foucault, Bataille, psychonahalyst Frend and other writer. Derrida received increasing attention in the United States after 1972, Where he influenced American literary critics and theorist more than academic philosophers.

Derrida's writing also concerns auto-bio-graphy. In 'Monolingualism of the Other' (1998). Derrida recounts how when he was in the Lycee and Vichy regime in France proclaimed certain interdictions concerning the native languages of Algeria in particular Berber.

For Derrida, a kind of purity remains as a value. In his 1992. The monolingualism of the other, Derrida speaks of his, 'Shameful intolerance' for anything but the purity of the french language. The value of purity in Derrida means that who conceives language in terms of proper or pure meanings must be criticized.

'Deconstruction' is the most famous of Derrida's terms. He seems to have appropriated the term from Heid egger's use of 'deconstruction' in Being and Time. Derrida has provided many definitions of deconstruction. But three definitions are classical. Simply, deconstruction is a criticism of platonism, which is defined by the belief that existence is structured in terms of oppositions and that the oppositions are hierarchical with one side of the opposition being more valuable than the other. Deconstruction is a kind of thinking that never finds itself at the end. Justice-this is undeniable, is impossible and therefore it is necessary to make justice possible in countless ways.

Course-XX (Option-III)
New Literatures

1. Claude Mckay
2. Rohinton mistry
3. Thumpa Lahiri
4. Maya Angelou
5. Kevin Gilbert
6. Jadith Ortis cofer
7. Alberto Alvaro Rios
8. Sipho sepmla
9. Yusef Kamunyakaa
11. Sherman Alexie's Reservation Blues

Claud Mckay

Claud Mckay (1889-1948) was a Jamaican writer and poet. He started writing poetry at the age of 10. He was educated by his elder brother, who possessed a library of English novels, poetry and Scientific texts. He was a communist in early life. At the age of twenty, he published a book of verse called Song of Jamica, recording his impressions of black life in Jamaica in dialect. Mckay was a substantial figure who emerged as one of the first and most militant voices of the Harlem Renaissance. He was regarded as one of the first major poets of the movement. Some of his most famous poems during that period were the Militant, If we must Die (1919) and his self portrait 'Outcast which was collected in Harlem Shadows (1922). He also wrote lyrics reminiscent of his Jamaican homeland and work about love and exile such as the 'Tropics in New York and Harlem Dancer. The tone for many of his works have been described as race conscious and revolutionary. He was an advocate for full Civil liberties and social solidarity. Mckay's pride in his culture and racial awareness helped stimulate expression in African American literacy.

In 1928, Mckay published his most famous novel, Home to Harlem' (1928), which won the Harmon Gold Award for literature. The novel which depicted street life in Harlem, would have a major impact on black intellectuals in the Caribbean. West Africa and Europe. The novel gained a substantial readership especially with people who wanted to know more about the intense and something shocking, details of Harlem nightlife. His novel was an attempt to capture the energetic and intense spirit of the 'uprooted black vagabonds". 'Home to Harlem' was a work in which Mckay looked among the common people for a distinctive black identity. Mckay also authored a collection of short stories, Gingertown (1932) and two autobiographical books A Long Way from Home (1937) and Harlem. Negro Metropolis (1940). His book of collected poems, Selected Poems (1953) and his second autobiography. My Green Hills of Jamica (1979) were published posthumously.

Losing faith in communism, he turned his attention to the teachings of various spiritual and political leaders in Harlem eventually converting to Catholicism.

Rohinton Mistry

Rohinton Mistry is considered to be one of the foremost authors of Indian Heritage writing in English. He was born on July 3, 1952 in Bombay. He is residing in Brampton, ontario, Canada. Mistry is of India Origin and belongs to the Parsi community. In 1975, he moved to Canada where he lived in Toronto and worked for a bank. He eventually returned to the University of Toranto to finish a degree in English and philosophy. It was while he was a university student in Canada that he began to write and publish fiction. His first two published short stories won the Hart House Literary Prize (1983 & 1984) and another story won the Canadian Fiction Magazine contributor's prize in 1985. Those three stories with eight others became his first book, "Tales From Firoszha Baag (1987). This collection of linked short stories concerns the inhabitants of an apartment compound in Bombay (now Mumbai). This book consists eleven short stories. It was later published in the United States as Swimming lessons and other stories from Firozsha Baag.

Rohinton Mistry's first novel, Such a long Journey (1991) brought him national and international recognition. The book concerns an ordinary man who becomes involved in the politics surrounding the bangladesh separatist movement in India and Pakistan. In 1998.such a Long Journey was made into a feature film. In Canada the book won the Governor General's Award for fiction and the W.H. Smith Books in Canada First Novel Award. It also won the common-wealth Writers prize for best book and was a finalist for Britain's Booker Prize.

Mistry's subsequent novels have achieved the same level of recognition as his first. His second novel, A Fine Balance (1995) concerns four people from Bombay who struggle with family and work against the backdrop of the political unrest in India during the mid 1970s. The book won Canada's Giller Prize, the Commonwealth Writers Award and the Los Angles Times Book Award. It was a finalist for the Booker Prize. Family Matters (2002) describes the members of a blended family who are trying to cope with the falling health of their father. The Scream (2008) has also won recognition.

Mistry's fiction deploys a precise writing style and a sensitivity to the humour and horror of life to communicate deep compassion for human beings. His writing concerns people who try to find self-worth while dealing with painful family dynamics and difficult social and political constraints.

Jhumpa Lahiri

Jhumpa Lahiri (1967) was born to Bengali parents in London, moved to Rhode Island, often vacationed in Calcutta during her youth and now lines on the border of Greenwich Village. After graduating from the Bernard College, she joined Boston University and attained Master's Degrees in English, Creative Writing and Comparative Studies in Literature and the Arts as well a Ph.D. Degree in Renaissance Studies. She also worked as a teacher in the same university. She started writing when she was ten years old. In an interview with Viphuti Patel she said, "When I learned to read, I felt the need to copy. I started writing ten page 'novels' during recess with my friends' writing allowed me to observe and make sense of things without having to participate. I didn't belong I looked different and felt like an outsider."

She has a number of awards in her credit. She won the 2000 Pulitzer prize in the year 2000 for her book "Interpreter of Maladies" which deal with the issues concerning the lives of Indians or Indian immigrants. A film was also released on the basis of her novel. The Namesake by the same name by Mira nair the first Indian to win the prestigious US prize as a Bengali Novelist.

Her personal life has greatly influenced her writing. She feels a strong attachment to her parents' Homeland as well as to London, as her birth place. But somewhere she feels a sense of homelessness and the same thing she shows in her works. She never feels belongingness to any country. She explains, "I didn't grow up there, I wasn't a part of things. We visited often but we didn't have a home. We were clutching at a world that was never fully with us". At a press conference in Calcutta, she also described the absence of belonging, "No country is my motherland. I always find myself in exile in whichever country I travel to, that's why I was tempted to write something about those living their lives in exile. The same idea of exile, we see in her Pulitzer Prize winning book Interpreter of Maladies. Her characters are struggling with the same feelings of exile and feeling turn between their two worlds. In her works, she displays the effect of displacement through her characters.

Recently Lahiri is chosen by New Yorker magazine to be among two dozen American writer below 40 who held the most promise for the new millennium. She feels fortunate that she was able to absorb the Indian Literature in a natural way. She says. :

"My parent never consciously set down and told me things about India, they sort of correctly assumed that I would learn things just by the virtue of being their child. I think it has always been important to them to maintain strong social ties with Indians living abroad and visiting India".

She inspires the writers by saying that try to write something everyday, but don't be too hard on yourself. Thus Jhumpa Lahiri is a wonderful distinctive new voice, who has been able to achieve something that most creative writer only dream of doing-writing all day.

Maya Angelou

Maya Angelou (1928) is an American authobiographer and poet who has been called 'America's most visible black female autobiographer' by scholar Joanne M. Braxton. She is best known for her series of six autobiographical volumes, which focus on her childhood and early adulthood experiences. She is an author, poet, historian, songwriter, playwright, dancer, stage and screen producer, director, performer, singer and civil rights activist. Angelou has been married for three times or more. In 1993, she recited her poem on the Pulse of Morning at the inauguration of President Bill Clinton, becoming the first poet to make an inaugural recitation since Robert frost at John. F. Kennedy's inauguration in 1961. She was the first African-American Woman to direct a major motion picture Down in the Delta in 1998. Although Angelou wrote her first autobiography I know Why the Caged Birds Sing (1969) without the intention of writing a series she went on to write five additional volumes. They are distinct in style and narration. All God's Children Need Travelling Shoes (1986), Gather together in My Name (1974), Singing' and Swinging' and getting' Merry like Christmas (1976) The Heart of a Woman (1981). Among her volumes of poetry are A Brave and Startling Truth (1995), The complete collected Poems of Maya Angelou (1994), Wouldn't take Nothing for My Journey Now (1993), Now Sheba Sings the Song (1987), I shall not be Moved (1990). Shaker, Why Don't you Sing? (1983), On Pray My wings are Gonna Fit Me Well (1975) and Just Give Me a Cool Drink of Water 'fore Divie (1971) which was nominated for the Pulitzer Prize. When I know why the caged Birds Sing was published Anglou was hailed as a new kind of memoirist. One of the first American Woman who was able to publicly discuss her personal life. Upto that point, black female writers were marginalized to the point that they were unable to present themselves as Central characters. The book has been criticized by many parents causing their removal from school curricula and library shelves. Parents and schools have objected to 'Caged Bird's depictions of lesbianism, premarital Cohabitation, pornography and violence.

Angelou used the autobiography to reimagine ways of writing about women's lives and identities in a male-dominated society. Her original goal was to tell the truth about the lives of black women and her goal evolved in her later volumes to document the ups and down of her own life. She is one of the most honored writers of her generation. She has been honored by universities, literary organizations, government agencies and special interest groups. She has been awarded over thirty honorary degrees.

Kevin Gilbert

Kevin Gilbert (1933-1993) was a 26th century Australian artist, poet, activist and winner of the National Book Council prize for writers. He was convicted in 1957 over the death of his wife during an argument and received a life sentence. Despite the harsh and brutal conditions of gaol life he learned printmaking and began writing. Gilbert wrote the play The Cherry Pickers in 1968 and first exhibited his artwork in 1970. During 1970s Gilbert became involved in numerous indigenous human rights causes. He wrote 'because a White Man'll Never Do It' in 1973. The National Book Council awarded his book 'Living Black : Blacks Talk to Kevin Gilbert (1977) in 1978. He was awarded the Human Rights and Equal Opportunity Commission's Human Rights Award for literature for editing the Aboriginal poetry anthology Inside Black Australia. He returned the medal citing the ongoing injustice and suffering of his people.

Gilbert uses the poetry as an apologia in respect to his own life whilst challenging the morality of the wider society as in Think (1971). His famous works are End of Dreamtime, People are legends, Black From the Edge (Non-Fiction) Me and Mary Kangaroo (For Children)

Gilbert's work has been included posthumously in numerous exhibitions. He communicated a vision for the way forward : "Only those who love the land and love justice will ultimately hold the land". He used his creative intelligence to cut through the layers of white denial that are the fabric of the foundation of Australia. He would often refer to his work as 'Tucker for the people'. The Slogan White Australia not a nation but a community of thieves was very much his theme for the years leading up to and including the 1988 Bicentennary. Raising our sovereign Flag was a particular favorite of Kevin's because it reflects the strength to be found in the unity of diversity.

Judith Ortiz Cofer

Judith Ortiz Cofer (1952) is an acclaimed puerto Rican author. She was born in Hormiguerous, Puerto Rico, moved to the United States in 1956 with her family to Paterson, New Jersey. She received an M.A. in English from Florida Atlantic University. She has written poetry, short stories, autobiography, essays, young Adult Novels. Some of her famous works are Peregrina (1996),The Line of the Sun (1989), Silent Dancing : A partial Remembrance of a Puerto Rican Childhood (1990), Cath the Moon (1996), The Year of our Revolution (1998), Sleeping With One Eye Open : Women Writers and the Art of Survival (1999), Call Me Maria (2004). In 2005, She published her most recent book, A Love Story beginning in Spanish : Poems. Among Cofer's more well known essays are 'The storym of My Body' and 'The Myth of the Latin Woman.'

Her narrative style is strongly influenced by oral storytelling, which was inspired by her grandmother, an able storyteller in the tradition of teaching through storytelling among Puerto Rican women. Cofer's autobiographical work often focuses on her attempts at negotiating her life between two cultures, American and Puerto Rican, and how this process informs her sensibilities as a writer. Her work also explores such subjects as racism and sexism in American Culturs, Machismo and female empowerment in Puerto Rican Culture and the Challenges diasporic immigrants face in a new culture. In September of 2009, it was announced that Cofer would be inducted into the Georgia writers Hall of Fame.

Once she said that "People ask me : If I am a puerto Rican writer, why don't I write in Spanish?", I respond that English is my literary language. The language of the country my parents brought me to Spanish is my familial language, that lies between the lines of my Egnlish language, Because I am a daughter of the Puerto Rican diaspora, English gives life to my writing.

In *The Global Education Project Cofer* wrote of her early years that, "I absorbed literature both Spoken Cuentos and books, as a creature who breathed up. I realized that the work was important to my being : To use my art as a bridge between my cultures. Unlike my parents I was not always straddling. I began crossing the bridge, travelling back and forth without fear and confusion." She herself confessed that Poetry is my emotional and intellectual connection to my heritage.

Alberto Alvaro Rios

Alberto Alvaro Rios (1952) is an American author. He was born in Nogales, Arizona a town near the side of U.S. mexicar border. Rios spoke both Spanish and English as a child. Rios started writing in the third grade although he referred to it as 'day dreaming." It was a secret act like speaking Spanish. He did not think his friends or family would understand him so he kept his writings hidden in the backs of his note-books and did not share with anyone until his teacher recognized his talent. He has written books on poetry, Short-stories and memoir. He is a Regents' Professor of English at Arizona State University in Tempe Arizona. His works of Poetry are : Dangerous Shirt (2009), The Theatre of Night (2207, The Smallest Muscle in the human Body (2002) which was nominated for the National Book Award, Teodora Luna's Two Kisses (1990); The Lime Orchard Woman (1988); Five Indiscrétions (1985); and whispering to Fool the Wind (1982) which won the 1981 walt Whiteman Award.

Her books by Rios include Capirotada : A Nogales Memoir (1999), The curtain of trees: Stories (1999) Pig Cookies and Other Stories (1995) and the Iquana Killer : Twelve Stories of the heart (1984), which won the western States Book Award.

Rios's poetry has been set to music in a cantata by James De Mars called "Toto's say," and on an EMI release, "Away from Home." His work has been included in more than ninety major national and international literary anthologies, including the Norton Anthology of Modern Poetry. He holds numerous awards, including six Pushcart prizes in both poetry and fiction, the Arizona Governor's Arts Award and fellowship from the Guggenheim Foundation and the National Endowment for the Arts.

Sipho Sepamla

Sipho Sepamla (1932-2007) was a contemporary South African poet and novelist. He was born in a township near Krugrdrop and lived most of his life in Soweto. He published his first volume of poetry, Hurry up to It I in 1975. During this period he was active in the Black consciousness movement and his 1977 book The Soweto I love, partly a response the Soweto Riots was banned by the Apartheid regime. He was a founder of the Federated Union of Black Artists and the editor of the literary magazine New Classic. He published several volumes of poetry and novels. He received the Thomas Pringle Award (1977) and the French Ordre des arts et des Letters for his writing. Sipho sepamla was posthumously awarded the literary lifetime Achievement Award at the 2007 SA literary Awards, Vodaworld, Johannesburg. His works are :

Poetry

1. Hurry up to It 1 (1975)
2. The Soweto I love (1977)
3. Selected Poems (1984)
4. From Goree to Soweto (1988)

Novels.

1. The Root is one (1979)
2. A Ride on the Whirlwind (1981)

Sepamla emerged as the supreme satirist of all his contemporary poets-Very comical too, Although comedy is never easy to pull off in poetry but sepamla did it. The anthalogy that best represented was 'To Whom It May concern'. It became his signal tune. The Soweto I love-is one of the few records in verse of the Soweto uprising that he set down, in the same manner he wrote of the Sharpeville massacre, as an eye witness. He fulfilled the role of poet as historian in those troubled times. The novel Ride on the Whirlwing was reissued in 2006 in a 30th anniversary edition. But the novel was soon suppressed in very strange circumstances. But Sepamla is best known for this novel.

Together with Oswald Mtshali and wally Mongane Serote, Sipho Sepamla is included among what has been called the poets of the big cities. These are their black satellites Soweto, Langa and Kwa Mashu. For a long time the new city poetry was self assertive, wrathful and disconcerting. What has distinguished sepamla from the other poets, however is his reluctance as concerns political rhetoric. He has used the black girl as a metaphorofAfrica and has provided us again and again with surprising images to sketch the South African situation.

Yusef Komunyakaa

Yusef Komunyakaa (1947) is an American poet. He was born in Bogalusa, Louisiana where he was raised during the beginning of Civil Rights Movement. He is the eldest of five children. He uses his childhood experiences to inform many of his works. His familial relationships, his maturation in a rural Southern Community and the musical environment afforded by the close proximity of the Tazz and blues center of New Orleans provide fundamental themes for several of his volumes. From his humble beginnings as the son of a carpenter, Komunyakaa has travelled far to become a scholar, professor and prize-winning poet. He is currently teaching at New York University and is a member of the Fellowship of Southern Writers. By the 1970s he had become one of the most popular and American writers of his generation. His first two volumes, Dedications and other Darkhorses (1977) and Lost in the Bone Wheel Factory (1979) were self-published. He first gained wide recognition for the collection copacetic in 1984.

His success continued with I Apologize for the Eyes in My Head (1986) which won the San Francisco Poetry Prize. He has published more collections of poetry, including Taboo; The wishbone Trilogy, Part I (2004), Pleasure Dome : New and Collected Poems (2001), Talking Dirty to the Gods (2000), Thieves of Paradise (1998), Neon Vernacular (1994) and Magic City (1992), February in Sydney (1989) Lost in the Bonewheel Factory (1979) He has also written dramatic works including gilmaesh : A verse play and slip knot.

In his poetry, Yusef Komunyakka weaves together the elements of his own life in short lines of vernacular to create complex images of life in his native Louisiana and the jungles of Vietnam. I Apologize for the Eyes in My Head takes the poet and his reader 'from lost love in the city to loved ones and friends lost to the evils of slavery and Jim Crowism in the deep South," adds Jones. In these poems, he continues his fascination with ghosts reflected in life's looking glasses with images of skeletons and with other symbols of mortality and life's fragility.

Sherman Alexie's Reservation Blues

Reservation Blues is a famous novel of Sherman Alexie. Alexie (1966) is an author, poet, filmmaker and occasional comedian. He lives in Seattle, Washington. His stories have been included in several prestigious short story anthologies including The Best American Short Stories. He is the recipient of numerous awards including the 1999 O. Henry Award, the 2000 inaugural PEN/Amazon.com short story Award, the poetry Society of America's 2001 Shelley Memorial Award and the poets and writers" Writers Exchange 2001" contest.

The novel Reservation Blues opens with Robert Johnson's arrival at a Spokane Indian reservation where he meets Thomas Builds-the Fire, who leads him to a woman who lives in the clouds that the blue singer has been dreaming about, Big Mom. This is no ordinary woman-She is reported to be hundreds of years old and incredibly wise. It is rumored that she even taught Janis Joplin and Jimi Hendrix. Johnson faked his death in 1938 and is under the impression that only Big Mom can undo the deal he made with the devil so many years ago. Thomas Builds the Fire takes Johnson to see Big Mom at Well point mountain and Johnson leaves him his guitar (which we will soon learn is no ordinary guitar) and Thomas sees his chance to form a blues band.

The band is comprised of misfits (including two native women named checkers and chess) from the reservation and they call themselves, 'Coyote spiring'. Mostly as a result of the charmed (or caused) guitar, Coyote springs begins to become popular with white people and they even gain two white groupies named Betty and Veronica who later become their own group who are constructed to look and seem Indian Furtheremore, they attract the attention of two men of cavalry Records named Sheridan and Wright 'who have names that parallel those of cavalrymen that slaughtered his people in the past). The plot of 'Reservation Blues' does not offer a traditional 'happy ending' tracing the rise and fall of the band provides Alexie the framework necessary for him toe discuss many issues relevant toe Native American—both past and present.

The Writer Sherman Alxie wants the readeu to think critically about the themes and issues related to Native American and reservation life. In this novel, Alexie has used the elements of outrageous fantasy to limn the realities of modern Indian life and not just Indian life because as Thomas Build the fire observes : "Ain't nothing gone wrong on the reservation that hasn't gone wrong everywhere else."

References

1. Usha Rani: *Psychological conflicts in the fiction of Anita Desai*, Abhishek Publications, Chandigarh, 2002.
2. M.H. Abrams. *A Glossary of Literary Terms* (Bangalore: Prism Books Pvt. Ltd., 1993).
3. Stephen Henderson, *Understanding the New Black Poetry* (New York: William Morrow and Company, Inc. 1973).
4. **Jean Wagner, *Black Poets of the United States* (Chicago: University of Illinois Press, 1973)**
5. **William Wordsworth, "Preface to *Lyrical Ballads*." English Critical Texts, ed. D.J. Enright & Ernest de Chickera. (Delhi: Oxford University Press, 1962)**
6. Kamala Das: *My Story*. New Dehli: Sterling Publishers, 1978.
7. David Daiches: *Critical Approaches to Literature* (New Delhi: Orient Longman)
8. Harr K.K.Ruthwen: *Feminist Literary Studies: An Introduction* (Cambridge University Press, 1984).
9. Blamires: *A History of Literary Criticism* (Macmillan India).
10. Brajesh Sawhney: *Studies in the Literary Achievement of Louise Erdrich, Native American Writer*: Fifteen Critical Essays (New York: Edwin Mellen Press, 2008)
11. James M.Cox (Ed.): Robert Frost: *A Collection of Critical Essays*, Spectrum Book

12. Robert P. Weeks (Ed.) *Hemingway: A collection of Critical Essays.* A Spectrum Book.
13. Bhim S. Dahiya: *The Hero in Hemingway,* New Delhi: Bahri Publicatoins.
14. John Gassner (Ed): *O'Neill: A Collection of Critical Essays.* Twentieth Century Views
15. K.K.Sharma (Ed.): *Indo English Literature:* Collection of Critical Essays
16. Arthur Miller, "Introduction to *Collected Plays*" (New Delhi: Allied Pub. Pvt. Ltd., 1973)
17. Sethi and Dhamija: *A Course in Phonetics and Spoken English* (Prentice Hall).
18. Nathaniel Hawthone. *The Scarlet Letters.* Peacock Books: Atlantic Publishers. 1993
19. Raghukul Tilak, *New Indian English Poets and poetry.* New Dehli, Rama Brothers, 1997.
20. W.K. Wimsatt, Jr. & Cleanth Brooks: *Literary Criticism* (Indian reprint by Oxford and IBH Publishing Co. Univ. Press
21. Robert Rubenstein: *The Novelistic Vision of Doris Lessing* (University of Illinois Press, 1979).
22. A.C. Baugh and T. Cable: *A History of English Language* (4th ed, London: Routledge and Kegan Paul, 1993)
23. O.P. Mathur *The Modern Indian English Fiction*
24. Roy Harvey Pearce (Ed): *Whitman: A Collection of Critical Essays,* Prentice Hall.
25. Richard B.Sewall (Ed.): *Emily Dickinson: A Collection of Critical Essays,* Prentice Hall.
26. Elaine Showalter: *A Literature of Their Own* (Princeton 1977).
27. Sandra Gilbert and Susan Gubar: *The Madwoman in the Attic* Yale University Press, 1979).